MW00583312

THE BOUNDLESS LIFE CHALLENGE

Adams Media
An Imprint of Simon & Schuster, Inc.
57 Littlefield Street
Avon, Massachusetts 02322

Copyright © 2018 by Simon & Schuster, Inc.

All rights reserved, including the right to reproduce this book or portions thereof in any form whatsoever. For information address Adams Media Subsidiary Rights Department, 1230 Avenue of the Americas, New York, NY 10020.

First Adams Media hardcover edition October 2018

ADAMS MEDIA and colophon are trademarks of Simon & Schuster.

For information about special discounts for bulk purchases, please contact Simon & Schuster Special Sales at 1-866-506-1949 or business@simonandschuster.com.

The Simon & Schuster Speakers Bureau can bring authors to your live event. For more information or to book an event contact the Simon & Schuster Speakers Bureau at 1-866-248-3049 or visit our website at www.simonspeakers.com.

Interior design by Sylvia McArdle
Interior images © Getty Images/charnsitr

Manufactured in the United States of America

1 0 9 8 7 6 5 4 3 2 1

Library of Congress Cataloging-in-Publication Data
Dillard-Wright, David B., 1976- author.
The boundless life challenge / David Dillard-Wright, PhD.
Avon, Massachusetts: Adams Media, 2018.
Includes bibliographical references and index.
LCCN 2018032004 (print) | LCCN 2018035227 (ebook) | ISBN 9781507208694 (hc) | ISBN 9781507208700 (ebook)
Subjects: LCSH: Attitude (Psychology) | Self-realization. | Change (Psychology)
Classification: LCC BF327 (ebook) | LCC BF327 .D55 2018 (print) | DDC 158.1--dc23

ISBN 978-1-5072-0869-4
ISBN 978-1-5072-0870-0 (ebook)

Many of the designations used by manufacturers and sellers to distinguish their products are claimed as trademarks. Where those designations appear in this book and Simon & Schuster, Inc., was aware of a trademark claim, the designations have been printed with initial capital letters.

THE BOUNDLESS LIFE CHALLENGE

90 days to transform your mindset~and your life

DAVID DILLARD-WRIGHT, PhD

adams media

new york   london   toronto   sydney   new delhi

CONTENTS

INTRODUCTION

Do you feel stuck in a rut in life? Are you looking to experience powerful and lasting positive change? Do you want to embrace meditation, mindfulness, and self-reflection, but have trouble integrating
them into your daily life? If so, *The Boundless Life Challenge* is for
you. I designed this ninety-day challenge to change your perspective,
encourage healthy behaviors, and open up new possibilities for self-
exploration.

What is "boundless living," anyway? It's finding everyday ways to
feel content. It's spending time outdoors. It includes meditating and
practicing introspection. It helps you figure out which of your habits
are working for you and which habits you need to leave behind. It's a
life in which you streamline your work, getting things done in a more
efficient manner. You will put aside time wasters and dedicate yourself
more fervently to your true purpose. Boundless living means finding
the wellspring of joy and spontaneity in your heart of hearts. By the
end of the ninety days, you will have a more positive outlook, practice
gratitude regularly, be more physically fit, and expand your horizons in
ways that make you happy. The benefits of this challenge will extend
far beyond the ninety days and into the months and years ahead.

Why a ninety-day challenge? First, it gives you enough time to truly
reflect and decide what areas of your life to improve. Yet, it's not *so*
long that it feels interminable. Second, you'll have a goal that's not
too far in the future (three months goes by quickly!) and daily motivation to help you reach that goal. Third, ninety days is a perfect amount
of time to build lasting habits that you can carry with you after the
time frame of this challenge.

The challenge is based on the idea that your mental landscape
affects your outer lifestyle and vice versa. In other words, you have
to have your inner house in order to make your outward-facing life
go smoothly. That's why this challenge works simultaneously on your

attitudes and affections as well as on the well-being of the body. The body and the mind are not two separate things but are part of one whole: the boundless life harmonizes mind and body, getting all parts of life synchronized and working together. To encourage that harmony, the four parts of the challenge are practicing gratitude, getting exercise and eating a healthy diet, engaging in meditative practices, and trying new things.

Remember that this life belongs to you: this is your world, and this is your time. Each and every hour of each and every day is precious, so make it count! To find happiness, we have to stop waiting around for better timing or better conditions. We have to stop thinking that things will be better when *this* or *that* happens. We alone are the guardians of our own fates. We make the lives that we want. As we learn to be more kind to ourselves, the whole world changes. The inner revolution brings the outer revolution. Self-love becomes the foundation for a renewed life.

What do you have to lose? Go forward full speed ahead, from day one. And that first day can be any time you like. It can be today, at the beginning of the month, or on a day with personal significance like a birthday or the anniversary of an important life event. Above all, begin!

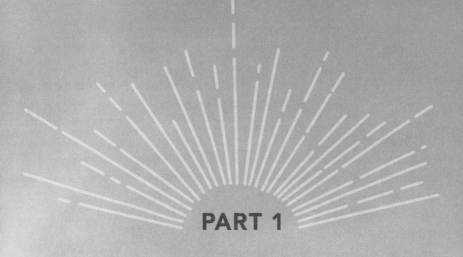

PART 1

STRATEGIES FOR BOUNDLESS LIVING

Those of us who are working for a boundless life have to learn to focus on the things that we can control, trusting that doing our own part will be enough and more than enough to take us to the place where we want to go. That place is one where we no longer have to live each day in fear, doubt, and worry. It is a place where we can give free expression to our ideas, where we can try on different lifestyles and personas without fear. A boundless life is a life in which we can choose our own destinies. We have the power to make our own fate, our own luck, our own way through the world.

This part will explain the specifics of the Boundless Life Challenge, then give you tips to set yourself up for success.

UNDERSTANDING THE BOUNDLESS LIFE CHALLENGE

The boundless life begins within your inner space, where pure possibility lies. When you live as your true self, you can envision a new life and then begin to fulfill your higher purpose.

The strategies for this challenge rely on an inner shift, going from believing that you have no control over your life to recognizing that you have resources at your disposal to make the changes that you seek. You go from believing in blind forces of chance to seeing that you really can control your own destiny. Where you had formerly engaged in self-destructive patterns of thinking, feeling, and action, you now begin to pursue positive thoughts and positive action steps. You calm the tumultuous inner life of thoughts and worries and seek the inner guide through silent reflection. You will find a new clarity and purpose, a desire for a peaceful and meaningful existence. You learn to take charge of that which you can control and let go of the rest. You accept responsibility for your life, and this sense of ownership brings new empowerment.

The four elements of the challenge all depend on one another:

1. Practicing positive thinking and meditative exercises for an hour total each day (you can break it up into smaller chunks of time if you prefer).
2. Incorporating gratitude into your daily life.
3. Engaging in healthy physical habits, like eating a nutritious diet and getting an hour of exercise every day.
4. Finding ways to have fun and expand your horizons, like trying new things.

The ninety entries in Part 2 will help you focus on these four goals in various ways. For example, on any given day, you might:

1. Identify self-limiting beliefs that have been holding you back.
2. Write down five things you're grateful for.
3. Get your physical activity outside, doing whatever activities appeal to you.
4. Foster your imagination in a fun way, like daydreaming or drawing.

As you go through this challenge, try to do one of the exercises in Part 2 every day, which will help you reach one hour of daily meditation or reflection. You might have time in the morning and in the evening, or sneak one into your lunch break. Abandon all thoughts that you are *doing it wrong* or that it *isn't working*. Your job is to simply do the exercises, not to police or judge yourself. Make sure to follow the prompts or nudges that you receive, but don't keep score in terms of the results that you see materializing. Again, your job is to simply do the inner and outer work; let the outcomes fall where they may.

Before you begin the challenge, take a few minutes to write yourself a letter, spelling out exactly why you feel that you need to make a change in your life. Be completely honest with yourself. Maybe you are feeling bored or depressed or tired all the time. Maybe you want to recover some of the happiness that you had during a special time in your life. Write yourself at least a page, or maybe three or four, explaining exactly why this challenge is important at this time in your life.

When you're done, tuck the letter away in a secure location; you are the only person who needs to know that it exists. If you ever feel unmotivated, read the letter to yourself. You will find the encouragement that you need in your own words, recorded by your own hand.

Take It One Day at a Time

Yes, this is a ninety-day challenge, but it is also a one-day-at-a-time challenge. If something sounds difficult, just commit to trying it for one day. You can do anything for one day, right? Then worry about the next day.

If you make a mistake, it is not the end of the world. Just try; try again. None of my suggestions should be taken as written in stone: take this book and adapt it to your own situation. (Just try not to modify it so much that you are no longer really doing the challenge.)

Remember also that diet, exercise, and meditation work in concert with one another. As you get better at one area of the challenge, you will find that the others get easier as well. As your habits get stronger week after week, you will find that it becomes second nature to practice some of these suggestions. There will be good days and bad days, but sticking with the challenge will get easier over time.

Dedicating Your Efforts

To spur yourself to complete this challenge with greater intensity, you might wish to dedicate your efforts to a person or cause that you find important. Maybe you would like to honor a departed loved one who supported you along the way. Perhaps you could dedicate your efforts to a teacher or mentor who means a lot to you. Or maybe you could pick a favorite charity and donate a dollar a day to that cause.

You might also consider posting to social media that you are completing the Boundless Life Challenge in honor of that person or cause. This sense of a larger purpose will help you to find your motivation when the going gets tough, as you will know that the challenge is not just about you. We are all part of one big, interconnected world. What we do in our own lives ripples outward to affect everyone around us. When we find our own inspiration, we become an inspiration for others.

Working in a Group

Some people might like to complete this challenge with a friend. You could invite someone you know or form a virtual group online. Just make sure to set a few ground rules. Keep the conversation uplifting and encouraging. Set specific goals and report back. If you mention a difficulty that you are having, you must be open to the suggestions for improvement that the group members have. See Appendix A for a complete guide to working on the challenge in groups.

Diving In

The rest of this part will help you meet the Boundless Life Challenge by giving you a toolbox of strategies that help you reframe your life in a more open-minded, positive way. For example, you'll learn how to:

- **Overcome learned helplessness**—start rejecting the idea that you can't change your life.
- **Trust that little voice inside you**—many of us find that voice drowned out by the world around us...it's time to begin listening again.
- **Make gratitude an inherent part of your life**—saying thanks for things big and small in your life completely transforms how you think about your place in the world.
- **Envision your future**—it's easy to become mired in your day-to-day responsibilities...but try to keep your mind open to all the possibilities out there.
- **Push past the boundaries that your ego sets for you**—your ego wants to maintain the status quo...don't let it.
- **Recognize and harness your personal power**—take control of your life using the exercises in Part 2.

These strategies will give you a boost when you're feeling a little down, serve as a guide when you're feeling lost, and empower you when you feel helpless. Feel free to refer back to them as needed as you work through the ninety days of the challenge and beyond.

OVERCOMING LEARNED HELPLESSNESS

The psychologist Martin E.P. Seligman pioneered some of the early work on learned helplessness. In one study that he describes in his book *Learned Optimism*, Seligman proved that helplessness could be taught to dogs via an experiment with shocks. Subsequent similar experiments performed on human beings proved that we, too, can learn helplessness. Outside the laboratory, a student who performs poorly in school for a few years may begin to generalize that experience and conclude that he or she is simply stupid. This person may take what amounts to something incidental and relatively minor and take it to be a defining and pervasive feature. Or suppose someone constantly tries crash diets, and they don't work. That person might say, "I just can never lose weight," rather than asking whether that particular approach was wrong.

In teaching philosophy classes, especially formal logic but really any philosophy class, I teach my students to be on the lookout for words like *always* and *never*, for black-and-white statements that admit of no exceptions. It is easy to spot bad arguments, because they are prone to sweeping generalizations. Children make this sort of argument. *I never get to go to the movies: it's not fair. He always gets to go first: no fair!* Funny how we spot this sort of thinking in children but not in adults. We say things to ourselves like *I've always been broke, and I'll always be broke* or *I've never been able to lose any weight.* Sound thinking would demand more nuance, but we normally let ourselves off the hook pretty easily, failing to call ourselves on our own nonsense.

The *always* and *never* statements rob us of self-efficacy, labeling as permanent what is merely long-lasting. In this way, we get off the hook for not putting in the effort to overcome the inertia of past habit. We have to shift from thinking that something is impossible to thinking that it is merely difficult. The path of action, even floundering action, will almost always be better than simply accepting an uncomfortable fate. The inexpert, faltering action at least has the merit of being an occasion for sharpening skills and gaining insight, while the person who fatalistically decides to do nothing has almost no chance at finding positive change.

A certain amount of pain and difficulty comes along with seeking a better life. You may fear falling flat on your face. You may feel ridiculous turning over a new leaf. Going into the gym or the art studio for the first time may make you feel awkward or self-conscious. It may seem as though all eyes are on you. Of course, this is just another illusion of the ego, but it feels real enough to be scary. Fear is the threshold that you must cross on the way to a new life. It is the companion on your way to claiming your own power.

In truth, you have always been very powerful, but certain negative ways of thinking held you back. You felt like you had to take care of everyone else but yourself, like you had to hold back on your gifts and talents so that you wouldn't stand out. The payoff for a belief in helplessness is a feeling of exemption from self-exertion. As long as you think that you don't have any power, it is not your fault if things aren't going well. The boredom, the sadness, the anxiety are simply default realities, the dull wallpaper of a tedious existence.

Yes, there is a pain in change, but there is also a pain in remaining the same. You get to decide what sort of person you want to be, whether to stay in your less-than-satisfying existence or move into something new. The good, exciting pain leads into a more abundant and fulfilling life, while the bad pain of stasis leads only to more of the same. In choosing to embrace this challenge, you have already affirmed that you believe that you are not helpless. You claim your own power to make changes in your life, to live the life of your dreams rather than passively going along with your previous reality.

TRUSTING YOUR INNER GUIDE

The Indian saint Sri Ramakrishna spoke of something called the *antaryamin*, the inner Guide or supreme Self, that, once contacted, would guide the spiritual aspirant toward the ultimate liberation in a swift and sure-footed manner. In ancient Greece, Socrates spoke of something similar—his divine sign, sometimes called a mantic sign—a kind of inner voice or feeling that restrained him when he was about to do something wrong. Some of us speak of something called the voice of conscience or, for the more rationally minded, the voice of reason. Others call it an intuition or hunch.

No matter what we call them, we all get these gut feelings on occasion. Unfortunately, sometimes we are too alienated from it, or we simply fail to heed its message. It's actually pretty easy to lose touch with your inner guide. The most common obstacle is simply the noise of civilization, the hundreds of web posts and podcasts, billboards and jingles that intrude upon your consciousness every day. Then there is the sheer pace of everyday life, which conspires against reflective awareness. We all have to make so many decisions so quickly that we don't have time to get in touch with the divine Self within. This harried way of life comes at the expense of peace and tranquility, and we often miss the valuable guidance that we can find by looking inside ourselves.

When we don't check in with the inner guide, we make inauthentic choices—choices that may not exactly be morally wrong in a universal sense but still conflict with our values. Failing to listen to this guide keeps us from living the sort of life that we want in our heart of hearts. When we deliberately attend to the inner guide, we receive hundreds of small nudges throughout the day, little choices that just feel right. These many small choices do not seem profound, but over time they result in taking us to a different place in life.

How to Hear Your Inner Guide

To get in touch with this guide, we have to cultivate interior silence, clearing away all of the mental clutter that makes it hard to hear the inward guidance. Here are two simple ways to do that:

- Take things slowly. Try to avoid frantic and impulsive behavior.
- Ask, "Is this what I really want?" or "What is the very best thing that I could be doing at this point in time?"

It's not that we are bad people or that we don't want to live according to our ideals; it's just that we sometimes settle for less than the best. We don't want the sort of direction that the inner guide offers. And yet, if we would learn to listen, the little nudges we receive are not all that difficult to hear. So often, the good choice is not much harder than the mediocre choice. This inner voice, the voice of the heart, is not a cruel taskmaster; it gently but steadily guides us toward our true selves.

We can consult the inner guide at any point and for any reason: for choosing which outfit to wear, for discerning how to spend the next paycheck, for deciding which friends are good influences. In order to receive guidance, we first must realize that it does not come from somewhere outside. The nature of the inner guide is not different from the nature of our true selves. In truth, we are already one with the deepest parts of ourselves. There is no work to be done. There is no Olympian height to climb. Calm and quiet are most necessary. Ramakrishna used the example of a fishpond. If you jump around acting all crazy, the mud on the bottom of the pond will be stirred, and it will become impossible to see through the water. But if you take very careful steps, the water will remain clear, and it will be possible to see the plants and the fish in the pond. The inner guide is kind of shy and reclusive; it will not appear when it is not welcome, and it will not appear in a very cloudy and cluttered mind. Once we have the inner calm, the guide becomes accessible and will be present all the time. The inner guide is absolutely steady and reliable, but it is very subtle. We have to want to receive its guidance and value its input.

Have you ever been in a situation where things just didn't feel right? Maybe you went to a party and things just felt *off*, or you went to a job interview and didn't feel good about the meeting. Maybe you went on a date and it went fine, but things just didn't *click*. Sometimes a situation can look good on the surface, and you can't point to anything objectively wrong about it, but you still aren't sure. This can be a sign that the inner guide is trying to speak.

Reframing Negative Thoughts with Your Inner Guide's Support

The inner guide can help us to reframe negative patterns of thought. It is easy to identify these thought patterns, because they lead us toward self-hatred and self-doubt. Some thoughts are just forms of self-torture. Usually these thoughts rehash all of the problems in our lives, or they begin with some variant of *I'm such a terrible person*. The thoughts that immediately precede self-medication are this sort of destructive thought. If you feel driven to drink (or eat, or take drugs, etc.), chances are you have just been practicing self-flagellating, self-destructive thinking. Take away the negative thoughts and you might just take away the need for self-medication.

The first step toward change is to notice the negative patterns of thinking and then to gradually replace them with kinder alternatives. We can think of the inner self as a glowing furnace of pure love, which is ready and waiting to destroy self-destructive impulses. As we begin to trust the true self, the afflictive thoughts and emotions melt in the radiance of the love at the center of our beings. That inner loving nature is there all the time, just waiting to be released.

In our heart of hearts, we don't *want* to practice forms of self-torture. We don't *want* to hate ourselves, and we don't *want* to hate other people. It's just that, when solutions seem absent in the outer world, we take up magical solutions in the inner world. We say to ourselves, by way of compensation, *if I can't change this situation, I will make myself feel miserable.* In the confused inner life, such compensatory actions make sense as a strategy to pursue when nothing else seems to work.

When we take a step back from self-destruction in the space of meditation, we see that sometimes doing nothing is better than the path that we formerly walked. Abstaining from harm is itself an action. Once we have abstained from harm long enough, creative solutions emerge that actually transform the situation. Getting in touch with the inner guide is the first step toward stepping back from the precipice of self-destruction and beginning to make a new way through life.

EXERCISING GRATITUDE

To create positive change in our lives, we must first become more aware of the positive circumstances already present. If we instead think of a negative situation, say a bill being late, and then begin to chain other negative things onto the first, things can deteriorate quickly. *I can't pay the bill; now my credit score will go down. Then I won't be able to buy that new car I need to get to work and I'll get fired.* Wow! That escalated quickly. See what happens when negativity goes unchecked?

Practicing gratitude is the exact opposite of the downward spiral of negative thoughts. We remind ourselves of the good things in our lives, and this becomes a self-reinforcing habit. We all go through difficult times, but we all have aspects of life to appreciate as well. Our minds, when they are not functioning properly, will tell us that everything looks bleak, but this picture is not accurate. We have to let a pinprick of light shine in. That little pinhole eventually widens, letting even more light shine into the inner space. We truly do have some degree of control in how we experience reality, even in the midst of the most difficult circumstances. We can pierce the gloom through the power of our own minds, even when exterior circumstances seem intolerable and out of control.

To practice gratitude, all you have to do is be willing to give it a try. Your inner curmudgeon will howl with ridicule. The sad sack version of yourself will try to hold you back. Your inner critic will prepare a thousand retorts and insults. In the midst of this onslaught, just calmly and patiently persist with the practice. Slowly but surely, your frowns will give way to moments of spontaneous joy. You will begin to experience change in areas of your life that you had previously regarded as permanently set into place. You will have a newfound sense of the efficacy of your own thoughts and behaviors.

In addition to working through the exercises in Part 2, try to spend ten to twenty minutes doing the following gratitude exercise every day.

The Daily Gratitude Exercise

It all begins with a breath. Settle into a relatively quiet place with minimal disturbances, sitting cross-legged on the floor or in a chair with your feet firmly planted onto the floor. Your hands may simply be relaxed in your lap or placed on top of one another, thumbs touching (*dhyana mudra* or *cosmic mudra*). Bringing attention to your breath, begin to lengthen your inhalations and exhalations. There are lots of methods of breath control (*pranayama*), but, for this exercise, simply lengthen your breath to four counts, or four times longer than the usual resting breath. Make the inhalation equal to the exhalation, pausing for only one count or less between breaths.

After a few rounds of deep breathing, the chatter in your head will probably become more obvious. You will have thoughts about various and sundry things and may be incapable of stopping them—that's okay. To try to quiet your thoughts, keep paying attention to your breath. At this point, become more aware of the outline of your body. Sense the boundaries of your skin, which may appear as a luminous envelope in the mind's eye. It is not uncommon at this point to feel a slight chill, a shudder, or a hair-raising feeling. The inner space comes to seem larger, more capacious. You may be able to sense the room in which you are sitting, all without leaving the inner space.

Next, move your awareness down the axis of your body. Go from perceiving the inside of your head to focusing awareness in your heart center, which may appear as a cave. Or it may appear as a more ornate structure, like a house or a temple. However you may wish to visualize the heart center, it becomes a quiet place of refuge. You may be able to sense the beating of your physical heart here in this space. Continue to observe the rising and falling of your breath.

Once your awareness has been centered in the space of the heart, cultivate a feeling of love. Nurture this feeling as strongly as possible, allowing love to radiate from your heart. You may picture it as a fire or as a light. Its glow pervades the heart region and reaches outside the confines of the body in all directions at once. Striving as energetically as possible, make this love as pure and boundless as you can imagine. Extend this love to yourself, to everyone in your life, and to plants and animals.

Continue to try to ignore the rush of your chattering thoughts, but intentionally allow certain thoughts to enter your heart center. Complete the sentence, "I am grateful for…," filling in the space with whatever comes to mind. Words and images may accompany the sentence completion (examples: I am grateful for my family, I am grateful for having a place to live, etc.). Repeat the sentence completion nine times, each time recalling something else for which you feel grateful. If nothing comes to you, don't worry; simply allow the sentence to remain uncompleted. Or you may wish to say something like, "I am grateful for this time of quiet rest."

Remember to continue with the deep breathing for the entirety of the exercise, as deep breathing is the quickest and surest method for reaching a meditative state of mind. Keep pouring the feeling of love and gratitude into each repetition of "I am grateful for..." There are no rules for what counts as a "correct" feeling of gratitude. You don't have to try to be noble or high-minded. You can be grateful for sex or a cup of coffee if that's what comes to mind. Just because something is earthly or bodily doesn't mean that it's bad. Everything is allowed; the important thing is to try to maintain concentration by focusing on the breath and the internal feelings of love and gratitude.

SEEING THE DESTINATION

Something led you to undertake this challenge: an unsettled feeling of some kind, a feeling that life is passing you by, that you wanted so much more from life. This feeling can manifest itself in many ways: as a desire for sound finances, for closer relationships, or for emotional well-being. Know that, whatever your desire, you can obtain exactly what you want and even more than you imagine. Life has many twists and turns in store for you, many of them mind-bending and unfathomable to you now. You may be thinking that you are too old to have the life that you desire or that you have already blown your opportunities or that your ideal life is too grandiose for you to actually achieve.

For the time being, simply set aside these doubts and disbeliefs. Imagine, just for now, that your life has much more in store for you than you can possibly imagine. Whether you are eighteen years old or eighty-eight years old, you still have a bright and bounteous future ahead of you that is filled with good things. You are endowed with pure and perfect potentiality, an energy of pure divinity that allows you to become whatever you wish. You are your own heart's desire, and you have everything you need within you. Just as an acorn holds within itself the potential to become a mighty oak, you have within your heart and mind the ability to become the person of your dreams and to have the life of your dreams. If anything, your dreams are a little too small and cramped right now. As you complete this challenge, you will begin to dream bigger, and, little by little, your actions will begin to fall in line with this bigger and bolder image of what is possible for you.

We visualize outcomes in our lives all the time. We think about conversations we have not yet had, mentally plan the route to work, and picture items to purchase at the grocery store. This ability to imagine and enact outcomes is very powerful, but, unfortunately, we don't take conscious control of this process most of the time. We fall into habitual patterns of action that, while effective in some sense, do not reflect our supreme good. Visualization exercises like this one allow you to dream an ideal life and then make the ideal a reality.

Visualizing the Boundless Life Daily Exercise

Try to take ten or twenty minutes a day for this visualization exercise. Begin with your breath. Take a deep inhalation, counting one, two, three, four. Hold your retained breath for a count of four. Then exhale for a count of four and hold for a count of four. (It's a sixteen-beat cycle: inhaling for four, holding for four, exhaling for four, holding for four.) Do this for at least four cycles before beginning the main part of the exercise.

As you do the breathing exercises, your inner space will come to seem more expansive. Bring your awareness down the axis of the body to the heart center. Your chattering mind will come to seem more peripheral and unnecessary. You will become more aware of the area surrounding your body. Picture an orb extending from your body about 4 to 8 feet in all directions. The orb is slightly oblong, so it is taller than it is wide; you may picture this orb, which is actually the energetic field of the body (often known as the *aura*), as a glowing light of white, lavender, baby blue, or pink.

The aura is nothing other than the energetic body (*pranamaya kosha*), a field of undulating lines of force. It is protective in nature, but it is not rigid like a suit of armor. The aura is womblike in nature: fiercely protective, maternal, and nurturing. As you sit in the space of meditation, see this protective covering supporting and nourishing your projects and endeavors. The divine energy of the Mother wants you to be healthy, happy, and prosperous. The Mother wants all good things for you. She makes Herself known in the crackling energy field surrounding your physical form.

Spend a few minutes tuning into the reality of the aura surrounding your body. When you feel established in its presence, begin to imagine the kind of life that you would like to have if all of your wildest dreams were to come true. Think about all areas of your life: career, relationships, finances, spirituality, and health. Where would you like to live in your ideal life? What would your social life look like? What kind of romantic relationship would you have? How would you spend your time and money? What sorts of meditative or spiritual regimens would you regularly practice? Make your visualization as real as you can, including sights, sounds, smells, tastes, and sensations.

Dwell in this space of pure possibility. Imagine the life that you would choose for yourself if there were no limitations, difficulties, or obstacles in your way. Picture the divine Mother taking control of the difficulties and moving them aside. Know that you are now crafting the blueprint for your new life and that the divine Mother will help you move from potentiality to actuality. The thought-forms you generate in the mind's eye will become your new life in due time. Your mind is a microcosm of the external universe, and, as you create things in the mental space, they soon become real in physical space.

Once you have completed your inner portrait of your ideal life, name three action steps that you can take to make your dream a reality. Picture the energy field surrounding your body protecting your plans from external and internal enemies. Self-doubt and negativity will not prevail against your endeavors. Criticisms and ridicule coming from the outside world will not hinder you in realizing your dreams. The divine love of the Mother simply absorbs and neutralizes all negativity as it enters your energetic body.

As you come back to normal waking awareness, the divine love enfolds you. You have a feeling of perfect serenity, knowing that you can and will make the positive changes in your life that you envisioned. Your heart glows with a pure and boundless joy as you believe completely in this power that you have within you to make your dreams a reality. You are cradled in the love of the Mother, and She will guide and protect you.

PUSHING PAST YOUR EGO'S DRAMA

The ego has a self-protective nature; it doesn't like change. The fact is that part of you would like to remain in the comforting confines of a narrow existence. You tell yourself all the time that you want change in your life, but the fact is that change is scary and requires effort. Before you get offended at the suggestion that you haven't really wanted the change that you profess to want, take an inventory of your fear. It is that fear of the unknown that keeps you locked in your present condition. Once you come untethered from fear, once you take that first step, all things become possible.

In case you have a hard time recognizing the ego nature, remember that it masquerades as your friend. The ego wants to prevent you from doing something that might hurt or embarrass you. On its face, this seems like a worthwhile goal. After all, it is not fun to fail at something. But a happy life demands that we exceed our previous boundaries, that we go from strength to strength, that we push past limitations. Risk is a necessary precondition to anything worth doing.

If we cater too much to the ego nature, if we listen to its advice, we get stuck in a rut. The ego nature leads to a safe but unsatisfying existence, characterized by shallow relationships and an emphasis on appearances. By contrast, following the inner nature leads to depth of feeling and an appreciation for life. An optimistic frame of mind aids in unleashing the inner, intuitive spirit, getting it out from under the crushing rationalizations of the ego. Pessimism is one of the tools that the ego uses to protect itself from the risks that arise from following the inner nature.

Pessimism is not really your friend; it is the enforcement mechanism used by the ego nature to prevent things from getting out of control. Pessimism is a buffer system that keeps you from feeling too deeply, that keeps you from thinking that you can change the world, whether that world is your own personal orbit or society at large. Pessimism keeps you cornered and powerless, unable to do anything whatsoever about the situations you encounter. When I say pessimism, I include its allied states, like self-doubt and cynicism. Pessimism underestimates the resources that we have at our disposal and overestimates the forces arrayed against us. It takes what might be a bad situation and makes it seem so dire that it cannot be overcome. Pessimism petrifies or fossilizes a fluid situation, making it seem more static and more negative than it really is.

Our inner, intuitive self, which I will contrast with the ego nature, wants us to gain new experiences, to enjoy all that life has to offer, to live in a bold and expansive way. The inner self doesn't care about embarrassment or failure; it just wants to have a rollicking good time out there in the world. It wants to meet people and go to parties. It wants to go kayaking, windsurfing, and rock climbing. It wants to sit in tranquility beside a still lake or on top of a mountain. It wants to look and feel like a million bucks. It wants to start new projects and learn new skills. It wants to visit new countries and try new foods. All of these things entail risk, which immediately causes the ego nature to try to put the kibosh on the plans crafted by the inner self. This tension between the inner self and the ego nature is the central dilemma of our emotional lives.

CULTIVATING PERSONAL POWER THROUGH THIS CHALLENGE

Each day, indeed every moment of every day, you have a choice. You can surrender to the censorship regime of ego and pessimism, putting your best plans on hold until more favorable conditions arise (they never do). Or you can ignore the ego's censorship and embrace personal power, by taking some small constructive action in the world—and that's what the daily exercises in Part 2 will help you do. Each day either expands or constricts your capacity to act, expands or constricts your belief in what is possible. The deliberate choice to be optimistic, to believe in your power, is simultaneously an expansion of the possibilities open to yourself and the world at large. You may not have infinite resources, but you do have true power at your disposal. It lies there at your fingertips, waiting to be used. You only have to say *yes* to life, to commit yourself to the continual process of striving and self-improvement, to forget about the past and move confidently into the future. Another world is possible; it is a world in which worries and anxiety are no longer masters. It is a world of plentiful supply for all of your needs. It is a world in which you take your best visions and make them into reality.

Sometimes we tell ourselves that it is more spiritual or more ethical to downplay personal power, to be humble and self-effacing, and, indeed, we do need to be wary of lording our power over others. But there is also an opposite error of hiding our own gifts and abilities in the name of false modesty. We can best serve others and be of use to the world when we claim the very real capacities and gifts that we have. We need to bring our A-game, for ourselves and simultaneously for others. To be our own "best selves," as Nel Noddings puts it, is to express our unique selves while also caring for those around us. As we care for ourselves, we cultivate personal power, and we put that power to good use by making the world a better place. We need to name as a false dichotomy the idea that we either take care of our own needs or look out for the needs of others. In order to be as effective as we might be, we have to both look out for our own interests and also achieve good things for those around us.

The ninety exercises you'll read next will help you to claim your personal power: to feel more creative and satisfied at work, to find joy and satisfaction in your relationships, to take care of your mind and body, and to recover a sense of spontaneity and enthusiasm. Allow yourself the gift of following this challenge. Look upon these ninety days as a luxury and not as a penance. Bask in the radiant glow of your own true Self, and walk confidently toward your chosen destiny.

PART 2

THE CHALLENGE: 90 DAILY EXERCISES

The following ninety days of exercises are the heart of this book. Completing them will change you for the better. We all have some bad lines of code, some viruses, if you will, in our operating systems. These bad lines of code are inherited from our parents, from society, from our friends and relatives. The computing metaphor helps us to think of these matters impersonally; in many cases, no one in our lives actually intended harm by introducing some element of self-doubt. Suppose you had an algebra teacher who made you come up to the board in front of the whole class to solve an equation, and your face turned beet red, maybe because you didn't know the answer. This experience introduces the thought "I'm bad at math," and this thought will remain there, unchallenged, unless you do something to counter it. Unless the bad lines of code are overwritten with better lines of code, the old program will continue to execute.

We can edit the code in our own minds by becoming better at introspection and then taking steps to correct the destructive ways of thinking and acting. As we have learned in an earlier chapter, meditation is a vital part of this process. We have to first be aware of the destructive patterns. But then we also have to take the additional step of countering the bad ways of acting with good ways of acting. And the most important thing to keep in mind is that thoughts and feelings are also actions that we can control. If we can learn to guide our own thoughts, we can learn to do anything.

The mind is the foundation from which our lives emerge. A broad-minded person inhabits a vast and interesting world. A small-minded person will continue to be a small person, no matter how much wealth and status that person acquires. We have to value our minds above all else.

1

Take a look at the limitations placed on your own life. You can discover these limitations by searching your mind for statements that look like this: *I can't do* x *because of* y. The variations are nearly endless: *I can't take a vacation to Paris, because I have too much credit card debt. I can't become a pastry chef, because my kitchen is too small. I can't read* War and Peace, *because I don't have enough time. I can't go parasailing, because my family will worry about my safety. I can't exercise, because I have bad knees.* In each case, there is something that you would like to do in your heart of hearts, and, in each case, there is some perceived obstacle standing in the way. These obstacles fall into a limited number of categories. First there are worries about resources—time, space, and money. The other obstacles generally pertain to relationships—the perception that a loved one will not approve of the new course of action.

Here's the kicker, though: these obstacles do not exist, or, if they do, they are not as insurmountable as they seem. These obstacles *lie within your own mind.* They are loosely based on the outside world, but they are not true reflections of the existing conditions. It's kind of like stumbling around your house in the middle of the night. For a second, you think you see a stranger sitting in the living room, but, when you turn on the light, you see only an overcoat tossed over a chair. There was something there, yes, but it was not anything to be afraid of. In the same way, we distort reality in our own minds so that we become stuck in our own patterns of living. As much as we might grumble about it, we like our old, comfortable habits. We like the obstacles, because they excuse inaction. It is easier to be stuck in unhappiness than it is to enact change.

To break this cycle, we have to defy the false perceptions by acting as if these perceptions of limitation and lack are not true. Do the positive things even if, in your mind, they would cause your loved ones to be unhappy with you. Spend the money for that new pursuit, even though you are afraid of not having enough. Find the time and space in your life for the things that you want to do, even though you are afraid that your work and home life will suffer.

Optimism provides the strength needed to move beyond fear. Repeatedly tell yourself that things are not so difficult as they might seem. Plunge yourself into uncertainty on a repeated basis, to trust that things will go well. When you are living in this way, it will feel scary but also exhilarating. There will be a feeling of butterflies in your stomach, a sense of giddy anticipation.

ACTION STEP

Today, examine the limitations in your life by looking for inner attitudes that take the form *I can't do* x *because of* y. Then act in such a way as to defy or contradict this rule that you have created for yourself.

2

If you really want to make progress at something in your life, it must be one of your top priorities. The problem is that we can only handle so many things at one time. To concentrate on one thing is, by definition, to ignore something else. Putting a project on the back burner is more or less the same thing as allowing it to languish. And yet we have to work within the constraints of our limited time and resources. So how do we reconcile these two things: first, the desire to be really awesome at something and, second, the reality of limited time and resources?

Once you have found an area of dissatisfaction, an area where improvement is desired, you have to bump up the priority level of that task, whether it is learning to speak French, building a scale replica of the Tower of London, or kayaking down the Mississippi River. The bigger the job, the more hours it will take to make it a reality. You can do the things you want to do by converting time and resources into the realization of that dream. Fifteen minutes a day will do, but three hours a day will be better.

The first adjustment is to reshuffle priorities so that the more desirable things get moved higher up the list. The second adjustment is to devote more time each day to the things that you want to flourish. This will also entail getting rid of the time wasters—the endless checking of email and favorite websites, the junk reading and junk thinking. Only you can determine what truly gives you enjoyment and what amounts to an addictive distraction. If it is truly detracting from your ideal life, it has to go.

ACTION STEP

Examine your use of time and make a list of three of your biggest time wasters. Decide to put aside your listed distractions for ten, thirty, or ninety days during this challenge.

3

Trying to improve our lives can be a lonely process; it is much easier to drift along with the crowd and take the path of least resistance. When we commit ourselves to optimal health and creativity, we will put ourselves out of step with mainstream consumer culture, which would much prefer that we remain couch potatoes and office zombies. Steering the direction of fate requires moving out of a passive role and taking charge of our own lives.

There is always the chance that no one will go with us when we step out and try something new. This can feel very isolating as we venture out into the unknown. Sometimes we have to build new support networks, composed of people who are involved in the same process, whether that might be a writing group, an entrepreneur network, or an athletic organization. We all need a few fellow travelers who are undergoing the same transformation.

The Boundless Life Challenge might feel like a solitary path, but really it is a movement of like-minded people seeking to improve their own lives and ultimately society as well. We seek to cultivate our own health and well-being, and we also look for a better world with more freedom of expression and holistic health for all people. This challenge is the beginning of a new movement that will make life better for all of us.

We live the boundless life each time we strike out in a new creative direction, each time we take care of our mental, physical, and spiritual well-being. We live the boundless life when we refuse to be governed by the past and practice self-care as a way of life. We live the boundless life when we practice gratitude. We live the boundless life when we refuse to be defined by other people and live into the deepest vision of our self-expressions. When we live the boundless life, we encourage others to do so as well.

ACTION STEP

Take ten to twenty minutes and write a few paragraphs about what the boundless life means to you, specifically. What habits, relationships, or thought patterns from the past do you want to leave behind? What good habits do you want to practice going forward? How can you take control of your own destiny and craft a better future for yourself?

4

Pessimism acts as a filter for our experiences: it keeps us from taking unnecessary risks, alerting us to threats in the environment. Pessimism also serves a useful evolutionary purpose: it keeps us safe and secure, wary of hucksters and scams. And yet, as human beings, we long for more than just safety. We want beautiful, fascinating lives full of both risks and rewards. If we protect ourselves too thoroughly through pessimistic thinking, we will also take away some of the hidden opportunities on the horizon.

Embracing an optimistic worldview also means increasing your tolerance for risk. It means that there will be a possibility for failure and loss, whether you are thinking about relationships, career, or leisure activities. But we cannot grow as people and cultivate our full potential without this nonzero chance that we will fall flat on our face. Safety and comfort are good, but they also make for a dull existence. Optimism allows us to get outside of our comfort zones, knowing full well that we may make a mess of things.

Oftentimes, we have a very narrow and limited view of ourselves based on our past experiences and the roles imposed on us by family and society. Failing an algebra class in high school doesn't make you *bad at math*, and it doesn't imply anything about the present state of your character. Likewise, skill in one area doesn't mean you can't have other talents; you can be both a nerd *and* a people person, both bookish *and* athletic. To improve the state of your life, you have to look at yourself in a more expansive fashion, to include those neglected parts of yourself. As you allow yourself to become well-rounded, your potential expands, and you throw away the limiting self-descriptions.

ACTION STEP

Have you been holding yourself back from some area of action in your life because of the fear of failure? Do you have a limiting self-definition that keeps you from living according to your full potential? Do something out of character today, something that challenges your ordinary view of yourself. See how it feels to embrace a more expansive definition of your abilities.

5

There is a difference between an ineffective complaint and a specific strategy for change. If I kvetch and grouse with my coworkers around the coffeepot about a particular problem at work, this will not be likely to create change unless this behavior is coupled with coordinated action. If I just whine to myself about a facet of my life that I don't like, this will be counterproductive unless I take concrete steps to improve the situation. A complaint is a value in disguise; it says something about how I want the world to be.

To become effective in creating the world that you want, you have to translate your complaints into values and then into action. For example, if I complain that I don't have time to exercise, I can translate that into the positive value of physical wellness. Then I can take action to ensure my physical wellness.

You have to put that value on the line by letting it inform your life choices. Once you allow the value to influence your everyday life, you have moved out of an inert and passive way of existence and into an active and resilient stance toward the world. You move away from pessimism and into optimism. You gain traction in the world through the skillful adherence to the values that you set for yourself. You move from taking life for granted to appreciating what you have.

Most of the time we don't think very much about the values that inform our lives; they exist somewhere in the background of our consciousness. They come into sharper contrast at times when one value conflicts with another or during periods of crisis and self-examination. Through conscious effort, we can become more aware of our values and play a more active part in how our lives unfold.

ACTION STEP

Take a frequent complaint that you have about some aspect of your life, whether it relates to work, relationships, or health. Now translate that complaint into a value. Finally, find an action that you can take today to express the value that you have uncovered.

6

Most of us have repeated, troubling scenes that recur in our lives. This could be a particular fight with a partner, perhaps about finances or chores. A recurring scene might be an ongoing dispute with a friend or trouble with addictive behaviors. We can push these repeated problems to the side or neglect them, only to have them return in a few weeks' time. We may come to have a fatalistic view of recurring problems, believing that they are insurmountable or that we somehow deserve them.

The pessimistic mindset clings to a belief in fate, the idea that the world is an ugly, nasty place and that we must continue to fight Sisyphean battles. Pessimism secretly embraces the drama that comes with fighting the same old battles over and over again. A pessimistic mindset, which has the ego at its core, loves the idea that some problems simply cannot be overcome, as this excuses inertia and inaction.

The optimistic mind takes a firmer stance and looks at the most difficult problems—even ones lasting perhaps decades—believing that these ongoing challenges can and should be overcome through diligent effort. Even in failure, the optimistic mind affirms that the effort has been worthwhile, because it is better to struggle and lose than it is to simply resign ourselves to a cruel fate.

ACTION STEP

See if you can recognize a repetitive, negative scene that recurs in your life. Now imagine what it would be like if you confronted the underlying problem in a decisive way, bringing your full powers to bear on the situation. What would you need to do so that you handle the situation differently, so that it doesn't keep returning? Take one small step in that direction today.

7

Many of us have scapegoats in our lives that we use to displace blame for the harsh circumstances that we face. A shallow psychological approach, for example, might lead us to blame our parents and our upbringing for our current problems. We might borrow some religious language to blame original sin or speak in philosophical terms of human nature—*I couldn't help it*, we tell ourselves. We might latch onto a conspiracy theory or strident political belief that seems to account for the realities that we face. Even more destructively, we may blame our intimate partners as they fail to meet our increasingly unrealistic expectations.

The most difficult step of all, the one rarely taken, is to accept responsibility for our own mistakes, to accept the consequences of our own past behaviors. An even more difficult action, but one that we must take in order to be free, is to accept responsibility without succumbing to self-hatred and self-destructive behavior. The boundless mindset accepts responsibility for past choices while also maintaining that the past need not determine the future. The optimist decides to change and does so, rejecting belief in the permanence of the past.

As we begin to understand ourselves a little better, we see that the mistakes we made in the past made sense at the time that we made them. We simply worked from incomplete information and partial advice, as one must do as a human being, bound by constraints of time and place. We cultivate compassion for ourselves, even as we reach for greater maturity. As we care for ourselves, we begin to make better choices going forward.

ACTION STEP

Who do you blame when things go wrong? Your parents? Your coworkers? Your friends? Your romantic partner? See if you are not placing unfair expectations on the people in your life. Inquire into yourself for the sources of the problems that you face. See if you can improve your own circumstances without relying on self-harming or self-medicating behavior.

8

It is an illusion to think that our own decisions alone determine the course of our lives; we will always have to contend with the prevailing social conditions, our socioeconomic circumstances, the geopolitical climate in our cultural moment. But there is also an equal and opposite illusion: the belief that we simply have nothing to say in our own unfolding potential, that we are somehow determined by forces outside of ourselves. It is very important that, if we are looking to change our lives for the better, we do not surrender the least bit of agency, that we own all of the power that we do have to change ourselves and our world for the better.

The reasons for doing nothing, for accepting mediocrity, either in ourselves or in our societies, are myriad. We can always tell ourselves that we have bad genes, that we do not have enough money, that so-and-so has it better and easier, that the world is just stuck in a particular pattern. These excuses are true enough—it's not that these factors of biography and biology are irrelevant—it's just that self-justifying excuses do not get us to the places that we want to go in life. But if we want to live larger, we have to ignore the voices of lack and limitation and forge ahead no matter what the difficulties may be.

Think about a professional climber ascending a steep wall of rock. The slightest protrusion in the face of the cliff provides a handhold, a toehold, the slightest bit of friction to make the climb possible. We just have to keep looking for those advantages, no matter how tiny they may be, so that we can build a better life for ourselves and others. It's never a matter of just being selfish: when I find the way, I show the way to others as well. Once an ascent has been made, it becomes an established route that others can follow.

ACTION STEP

Take one of your personal goals, whether it is related to health or spirituality or activism, relationships or hobbies. It could be a large or small goal; the size doesn't matter. Instead of thinking about all of the obstacles in your way, think of all of the resources at your disposal. Make a list of the small steps you can take today toward your goals.

9

In engineering, the term *latency* refers to the lag time between the sending of a signal and its reception, or the time between a cause and an effect. In online gaming, for example, a player with a very high connection speed will have an advantage over a player with a slower connection, an advantage that has nothing to do with skill. In online trading, latency in the software could make a tremendous difference in how much money a trader or corporation can make, with millions of trades taking place in fractions of a second. In today's world, rapid execution makes all the difference.

Today, work on reducing the time that you take between realizing that something needs to be done and actually completing the task. Don't make a project out of the small things—get them done as quickly as possible, without too much mental entanglement. If a job doesn't require a lot of reflection, just do it automatically. For the midrange tasks, the ones that require some concentration and planning, stack them in order of importance and execute accordingly. And make sure to spend at least some time every single day on the very large projects that are important in your life.

The key point for today is to reduce the lag between seeing that something needs to be done and actually doing it. As you stop laboring over the little things, you will reduce mental and physical clutter in your life. You will have a much better idea of what you should do at any given time. Make a habit of asking yourself what level of attention each task deserves, and allocate your resources accordingly.

ACTION STEP

Make yourself a to-do list of everything in your life that needs to be done. You will initially notice an anxious feeling. Now tag each item according to the amount of time and attention that you think each item will take. By the end of the day, try to do some jobs from each category. You will notice that your anxiety begins to wane as soon as you get started.

10

Our destinies are intertwined with every other creature on the earth. When we harm nonhuman animals, we become less caring and compassionate individuals. We lose a little bit of the sensitivity and concern that makes us fully human. Being born into a human body does not make us the lords of the earth, free to dispose of the planet however we want. A good future for the human race must also include a good future for all living things. If we are to survive and thrive as a species, we must take more seriously the needs of all the creatures of the world, from the tiniest plankton to the whale.

Making dietary changes can be a good down payment toward a more sustainable existence. You might consider eating less meat or protecting the habitat of a creature you particularly like. As we change our behavior related to the things that we purchase and put into our bodies, we also change the world around us. We support the sorts of stores and the sorts of companies that we would like to see thrive in the global economy.

We can make all kinds of changes that lead to a more sustainable future on the planet. We can investigate our investment portfolios to divest from polluting industries. We can carpool to work, ride a bike, or use public transit more often. We can switch to more efficient appliances and install solar panels. We can support political candidates who make the environment and conservation a priority. None of these changes happen overnight; they are long-term, lifestyle commitments that require advanced planning. The sooner we begin, the better the future will look for humanity and for the planet.

ACTION STEP

If you are a long-term meat eater, try to go for a day, a week, or the duration of this challenge without eating meat. If you are already vegetarian, see if you can eliminate eggs or dairy for part or all of this challenge. If you are already vegan, see if you can find ways to reduce your carbon footprint or food waste (for example, by composting or carpooling).

11

Our bodies have about 700 muscles, which we can use to twist and bend, run and jump, shout and climb. Unfortunately, we usually only move our bodies in very restricted ways, hunched over keyboards and machines for most of the day. Our bodies bear the marks of this strain, with chronic back pain, carpal tunnel syndrome, and muscle and skeletal weakness the inevitable result. We also suffer from heart disease, diabetes, and stroke, in part due to poor diet and insufficient exercise. In the developed nations of the world, we claim to prize our freedoms, but we don't actually exercise one of our most important liberties, that of moving around in the environment.

We spend most of our time in the house, followed by time in the car, followed by time at a desk. This stunted routine is not much different than what would be allowed under house arrest ordered by a judge! To break the cycle of debilitation that accompanies this routine, we have to move our bodies and explore our surroundings. This requires getting outside and engaging in physical activity on a daily basis. Physical activity is not just good for us in a physical sense; it also contributes to our mental and spiritual well-being. We are creatures born of the earth, and we must live as creatures of the earth in order to be well.

Those who desire the boundless life make it a point to spend at least some time every day in the out-of-doors, seeing what the body can do when its full potential is unleashed.

Exercise is not some sort of chore to be performed mindlessly; it is an expression of our humanity, an outcome of the freedom of our spirits. If we want to be intellectually and emotionally liberated, we also must use our bodies as vehicles of expression.

Whether you climb or run, cycle or dive, run or swim, dance or leap, you should put all of your spirit into what you do physically. As you get your body moving in your surroundings, you will also think in new directions and discover new experiential horizons. As you explore the potential residing in your body, your lived realities become richer as a result.

ACTION STEP

Go outside for at least one hour today to engage in some sort of physical activity. To prevent repetitive motion injury, mix different types of activity with different levels of intensity. Try not to do the exact same activity two days in a row.

12

The self-storage industry in the United States is worth almost $40 billion. Think about all of the millions of acres of space devoted to storing the crap that people no longer want or need. Think about all of the money spent on simply storing unused possessions that could be put to more productive use. We could all do with a little more simplicity in our lives. We could stand to be a little more selective about which possessions we allow into our homes.

Marie Kondo, author of *The Life-Changing Magic of Tidying Up*, writes that "when you put your house in order, you put your affairs and your past in order, too." When we subtract the things from our lives that we do not find valuable or meaningful, we create space for new things that truly bring us joy and meaning. We can also reserve some empty space for contemplation, so that our minds are not disturbed with excess clutter. A storage unit might be a temporary solution for a move to a new city, but it is not a solution for a lack of mental clarity. We can clarify our life's purpose by being careful about the books, clothing, and gadgets that we bring into our physical space.

Let's say that you really love books. The last thing you would want to do is to dump every title into the rubbish bin. A better approach would be to sort through each shelf, subtracting the titles that are simply taking up space. Do you really need to save every beach read, every airport diversion? Keep only what feels personal and special to you, the books that made a difference in your life, that stay with you after many years, that you would recommend to a friend.

We can use this method of subtraction to organize any space, whether it is a bedroom, a kitchen, or an office. Some people may have a hard time doing this, because they suffered want in the past or perhaps have personality issues. The extreme cases may require help from professional organizers, but most of us can just take a deep breath and begin. This may not be the most fun way to spend an afternoon, but it does pay big dividends in peace of mind. It also allows other people who may be less fortunate to make use of possessions that are going to waste.

ACTION STEP

Today, pick one space and declutter it. This does not have to be a whole room; it could be one cabinet, one drawer, or one shelf. You might also choose to clean your car or just the trunk of your car. Take the unwanted items and donate them right away.

13

If you have ever made a vision board or practiced the law of attraction, did you find the experience to be invigorating or frustrating? It can be disappointing to try some new technique for realizing a goal or finding abundance, only to have it fail spectacularly. The knee-jerk reaction to such failures is sometimes to never attempt positive change again. But it's much more productive to instead look at the causes of our failures and get more clarity about why our well-laid plans do not come to fruition.

Perhaps we did not really want the thing that we thought we simply had to have. If you are studying for the CPA exam but do not want to be an accountant in your heart of hearts, chances are you will find reasons to avoid hitting the books. If you are saving for a trip to Peru and somehow those funds don't materialize, maybe you really want to go to Spain or India. The goal must really be inspiring to catalyze change. We have to make sure that we are not living in someone else's dream, that we are very excited about the new reality that we want to see realized.

Sometimes a desired outcome does not materialize because we didn't put in the necessary time and resources to make it happen. If I want to learn to speak a foreign language fluently, listening to an audio program on the daily commute will be a good start, but it won't get me all the way to the goal. That requires something close to complete immersion. Half-efforts usually won't be enough to realize a goal that is something close to a lifelong pursuit or a life goal. We have to be honest with ourselves and recognize the magnitude of what we want to achieve.

And at other times, life will intervene. Sometimes things happen that we cannot control. It would be unreasonable to expect that our plans will be unaffected when something major like this happens. We have to be willing to be flexible, to change with the circumstances. It is important to not be too hard on yourself when plans do not come to fruition. Simply set that attempt aside and start again with greater clarity and renewed energy.

ACTION STEP

Think of a failure from your past that still bothers you. See if you can identify the source of the failure. Were you living in the wrong dream? Did you fail to commit enough time and resources? Did life just get in the way? See if your old passion is worth renewing or if you just need to let it go. Commit either to beginning again, with new insight, or to releasing the hold that the past has on you.

14

As I think back on the students that I have had in college classes in philosophy over the years, only a small percentage actually failed my classes. Normally the students who don't succeed actually have the intellectual ability and the material resources to do the work. The reasons for failing have nothing to do with lack of talent and everything to do with life habits. Addictions figure prominently: alcohol and drugs, or even video games! Success in college, just like success in all areas of life, requires putting aside certain behaviors and sitting down to do the work.

Most people are addicted to something, and for some people, addiction rises to the level where it should be treated as a disease. We are not responsible for our genetic predispositions, but we are responsible for getting help when we know that we need it. Addiction is like a bottomless pit that sucks away all of our time and money. Eventually, it also takes our relationships, from romantic partners to family members to good friends. Addiction affects people who have already lost it all as well as those who still have it all. Living the boundless life, which is a life of ease and grace, requires facing addiction. We don't have to be perfect to live the boundless life, but we do have to confront our demons directly.

Every addict thinks that his or her own behaviors are no big deal and that other people are the ones who really need help. It requires a lot of courage to look within and see that a change needs to be made. It requires courage to admit that we may have harmed our friends and relations because of our behavior. Whatever may have happened in the past, each day is a chance to start again, to put the old ways behind us and build a better future. The resources once put toward servicing the addiction can be put toward interesting projects and plans.

ACTION STEP

Write down all of your addictions on a scrap of paper or an index card. These addictions could be anything from checking email to buying lottery tickets to drugs and alcohol. Put a check by each item that you feel like you have to do every day or several times a day. Put another check if that item sometimes or usually interferes with relationships in your life. Put another check if the item ever interferes with your ability to make a living. Put another check if the item reduces your happiness in life. If you have more than one check beside any item, make a plan for addressing the addiction. Start by abstaining from that compulsive behavior just for today, and then challenge yourself to put aside that behavior for the rest of the ninety days of this challenge.

15

We all have a tendency to look for the "big breaks" that will really make a difference in our lives. The truth is that the little things we do every day make much more of a difference in who we become than any one monumental event. When we have our working habits down pat, when we do our little bit each day, the external rewards have a way of taking care of themselves. That's why it is so important to get into good patterns: getting enough sleep, eating decent meals, exercising regularly, and working in a disciplined manner. This is the basic, tortoise-versus-hare lesson that is not very sexy but is very effective.

We have a tendency to think that we need big blocks of time to get anything done—four hours here, a day there—but that is not a reality for most of us. If you are sitting on a big idea, waiting for that magical disruption-free afternoon, wait no longer. Fifteen minutes or an hour will do. Take your idea and get it down on paper in the form of a business plan, a book proposal, or a series of sketches. Then make a plan for bringing your project to completion. Keep stealing little snatches of time until you have a working prototype. Then continue to refine until you have something wonderful.

Some of us will not have the luxury of being able to pursue our creative projects full time, but that doesn't have to be a deterrent. We can still get things done through persistent daily effort. This method does not guarantee success, but it does guarantee that your idea will at least make it into a workable form that sees the light of day. Most blocked creatives are full of ideas, but they don't have anything to show for it. Productive creative people know that ideas are easy but execution is difficult. That is why working creatives place a premium on completing the process, not just generating ideas.

ACTION STEP

Do you have a creative project that you moved onto the back burner? This project could be anything, from composing a song to writing a short story to making a video. Get to work on your project for at least fifteen minutes today. Then find time for your project whenever possible for the duration of this challenge.

16

Oftentimes, we allow ourselves to be content with less than the best. For years, I wore ill-fitting clothes in a drab color palette, just because I thought that's what other people expected me to wear. I also thought that I didn't have enough money to invest in a new wardrobe. When it came to my fashion sense, I just soldiered on, discontent with my appearance but also unwilling to change. Eventually it got to the point where it was depressing to even open my closet, and I had to begin to invest in a new look. I suddenly had a lot of learning to do, as I began to experiment with new colors and styles.

Those of us who have an intellectual mindset can be tempted to ignore physical appearances, but how we are perceived on the outside has a big effect on how we feel on the inside. There is no inner self that can be strictly opposed to the outer self. This is why we have to take steps so that our appearances match how we feel. Otherwise, we begin to feel miserable in our own skins; having an appearance that doesn't match our true preferences takes a big psychic toll.

We cannot all afford to hire personal shoppers and stylists, but we can be more careful about what we buy and what we wear. A good fit makes all the difference in the world, followed by good color choices. If they don't look and feel great, the clothes shouldn't ever come home from the store. The same goes for online purchases: don't keep something just because you don't want to go to the trouble of returning it. And you don't have to change everything at once: just replace one outfit at a time until most of the ugly or ill-fitting items have been removed.

ACTION STEP

Go into your closet today and look for items that you hate to wear. Put them into a bag for donation, and do so without reservation or regret. Then spend half an hour shopping, either online or in person. If you find something you love, buy it if at all possible. If you don't find anything you absolutely love, walk (or click) out of the store empty-handed.

17

Money may not be able to buy happiness, but it can cause a lot of heartache if it is not managed properly. Financial problems drive a large percentage of divorces and mental health problems. But managing money need not be a cause for panic or alarm. For those of us who are not particularly skilled in this area, managing money is a standard chore, like taking out the recycling. The second I use the word *chore*, you may feel immediately turned off. But here's the thing about managing money: if you take care of it, the money will grow. And that makes money management a special sort of chore, one that actually pays you back!

We all have a lot of financial stressors in our lives, from paying the rent or mortgage to covering all of the utilities and insurance to saving for college and retirement. Life is very expensive, but there are also a lot of tools available today to make things easier. Personal finance apps help us to track where each dollar is going, and many investment sites make it easier for nonprofessionals to manage a portfolio of stocks. Even keeping a simple checklist of monthly bills on paper can make the difference between a financial mess and a decent situation.

Don't be afraid to delve into that stack of bills and see what's happening. If you get into a panicky mode around money, you're more likely to make bad choices. It is best to take a deep breath and then calmly and patiently see what's coming into your coffers and what is going out. By exercising a little daily effort, you can make big improvements in your financial life.

ACTION STEP

Take a few minutes today to make sure that you know the exact balance in your accounts, as well as any automated withdrawals that are soon to be deducted. If you have not already done so, make a list of all the bills that you pay each month. Make sure you know the deadline for each payment, and try to pay each bill on time. If you already have such a system in place, spend a few minutes looking for new investment opportunities.

18

So often we take for granted the people in our lives who make each day worthwhile. Whether that might be a significant other, children or grandchildren, friends and neighbors, or the barista or checkout person, we sometimes forget to smile and say thank you. As we get immersed in our daily routines, we forget the contributions that these special people make in our lives. We become inured to the importance of one-on-one contacts, those ordinary, everyday interactions.

The person sitting one desk away or the person next to you in the checkout line at the store could be needing a little bit of a pick-me-up today. One kind word from you could mean the difference between a good day and a bad day. The little kindnesses that we show each other ripple outward in all directions, making the world a better place to live. Let's get out of our own heads and pay a little more attention to those around us.

If you have ever worked as a server in a restaurant, you know exactly what I'm talking about. On the days when the customers are kind and generous, the job is pretty enjoyable. But on the days when the customers make all sorts of unreasonable demands (and tip poorly!), the job is an unforgiving grind. A little bit of kindness and generosity goes a long way.

ACTION STEP

Today, try to be mindful of the people in your life. Write a little love note or text to your significant other. Put a tip in the jar at your coffee place and say thank you. Say hello to random strangers and be a little more outgoing.

19

Americans spend, on average, about $200 per capita each year playing the lottery. When you take into account the fact that a lot of people don't play at all, that's a lot of dollars going down the drain. We can better spend our money giving ourselves the small luxuries that don't cost much money. A nice new set of sheets, a manicure or shave, some new bath products: these are all ways to treat ourselves without breaking the bank. Taking the time for self-care creates a more positive state of mind that allows us to feel more at home in our own lives.

You may find yourself feeling a little guilty about these self-indulgences, a small voice inside your head that tells you that pampering yourself is wasteful or frivolous. But think for a minute about the things that you do for other people: the way that you take care of clients and customers, your family members, your companion animals. You deserve the same care for yourself that you extend to other people. When you care for yourself, you are better able to do things for others without feeling resentful.

The emotion of guilt often arises when we take care of ourselves. We can feel selfish for taking care of our own needs instead of taking care of others. The guilt emotion is a false indicator, like an instrument on an airplane that is no longer functioning. The feeling of guilt, by itself, cannot tell us whether something is right or wrong; it is simply too prone to false positives and too skewed by our backgrounds.

To get rid of this feeling of guilt, we have to tune into our bodies more deeply. What feels good to the senses isn't necessarily wrong. I'm not talking about *overindulgence* here; I only want to highlight the sensual side of life. We can find comfort in the feel of a soft fabric, in the fragrance of a nice bouquet, or in the therapeutic touch of a massage. There is no harm in such indulgences. They help us to appreciate the beauty in life and to feel glad that we are alive.

ACTION STEP

Find some way to indulge your senses today, whether you purchase a handmade soap, give yourself a massage, or listen to some good music. Set aside all distraction, and get fully in tune with the experience. If the guilt emotion arises, don't let it deter you.

20

Do you have someone in your life you would like to get to know better, someone at work or the gym or a friend of a friend? Maybe you admire that person's fashion sense, or maybe he or she has an interesting hobby. Maybe you admire this person's sense of humor or flair for conversation. I'm not talking about romance here, necessarily; this admiration could be completely platonic. Chances are, when we have this friendly sort of admiration and appreciation, it means that this person has lessons that we need to absorb in order to grow as people.

We are formed by our relationships. The people who surround us point the way toward new interests and inclinations. Or they may influence our characters, helping us to be more forgiving or gracious, more lighthearted or witty. Or they may hold up a mirror to our lives, allowing us to see our problems from someone else's perspective. As human beings, we are social animals—everyone needs at least a few social contacts in order to remain emotionally healthy.

It can be hard to make friends as grown-ups. Work and family consume most of our time, and it can be tempting to spend what little free time we do have watching Netflix on the couch. As hard as it may be, we have to try to maintain some friendships even though our lives are filled with responsibilities. Otherwise, we get isolated and myopic, bound to our own limited perspectives on the world. Friendships help us to see things that we simply cannot see, the little blind spots that keep us from living our full destinies.

We don't have to be purists about it; a friend at work or a meaningful online friendship will do. Everyday chitchat is also valuable. We can't bare our souls to another person without first talking about sports or the weather or some other mundane topic. We have to begin where we are and work on making stronger connections with people. For introverts especially, this is a big job, but it has to be done in order to find the boundless life that we are all meant to have.

ACTION STEP

Do you have someone in your life who you would like to get to know better, someone you admire? This could be someone you barely know, or it could be someone you already consider to be a friend. Take the time today to get in touch with that person and ask them if they want to get coffee or lunch. Put the date on your calendar and keep the appointment.

21

To really change our lives, we have to be willing to take a long, hard look at ourselves, to ask how we contribute to our own sense of feeling stuck in life. As long as we blame society or our parents or the government or any other favorite scapegoat, we excuse ourselves from having to do the work of transformation. Change begins the moment we take ownership over our own lives, the moment we accept responsibility for our choices and become willing to do things differently. No amount of self-pity will ever take the place of the slightest shred of initiative.

Getting off the couch and getting things done may lead to failure, to be sure, but a noble failure is worth much more than apathetic floundering. Failures teach us more about ourselves than we knew before. We get a better sense of our strengths and weaknesses. We realize what works and what doesn't. We test ideas and refine them. We learn by doing, not by blaming others for the things that go wrong. This process of risk-taking begins with the simple decision to try something and see what happens.

What's more, when we ignite the fires of passion within ourselves, we naturally attract others to the cause. No one ever really makes it alone. But drive, passion, and intelligence help in attracting the right team and keeping that team going. If we don't first believe in ourselves, no one else will either. When we purposely cultivate belief in ourselves, we jump-start our projects and plans.

It can be hard to overcome years of self-doubt. The journey begins by practicing deliberate self-love. I am talking about genuine self-love, not the sort of shallow narcissism so prevalent in our culture. We have to look at ourselves clearly, seeing every perfection as well as every flaw, and build as much love as possible. We build this feeling of love for ourselves, and we also direct it out into the world, to the people we encounter each day. This love of self and others is a strong force that is capable of expanding our horizons, pushing us past old limitations and into unexplored territory.

ACTION STEP

Take some area in your life where you have been feeling stuck. Now ask yourself what you previously were not willing to do to improve that area of your life. Decide today to do one thing differently, to exert a little more effort or try a different tactic or commit more resources.

22

No matter what career we choose, whether working as a carpenter, a nurse, a cashier, or a lawyer, we should try with all of our might to put our creativity and individuality into our efforts. Even the most demanding of workplaces still has a tiny bit of wiggle room for free expression, and we should take that little space of freedom and do something beautiful with it. The temptation will always be to turn ourselves into cogs in the machine, to make ourselves fit the job instead of making the job fit with our personalities. A business that does not serve people, including its employees, deserves to be replaced with a more humane and refined competitor.

Rather than making ourselves conform to a business beige sort of blandness, we should allow ourselves our quirks and randomness, testing the boundaries of corporate culture rather than allowing corporate culture to dictate our personalities. Rather than predetermining the sort of persona that we think will be advantageous, we give expression to the self that wants to be born within us. When we try to live according to other people's desires for us, we lose sight of our uniqueness. Living according to that uniqueness yields a feeling of freedom and release.

We have to keep a lookout for self-censoring behavior that stifles our spontaneity. Self-censoring means always thinking about how others will feel and think. There is nothing at all wrong with being thoughtful and empathetic, but sometimes a desire to please others crosses the line from being simply kind to being self-effacing and even self-damaging. We should also give people credit; sometimes they can be more resilient and understanding than we know. If we go around walking on eggshells, it can be hard to find the truest expression of our personalities.

You don't have to conform yourself to someone else's mold or live in someone else's dream. We are not guaranteed tomorrow, so we have to live our best lives today. That means packing as much joy, as much laughter, and as much play as we can into each and every hour. Life is not meant to merely be endured; it should be a celebration of all that we hold dear. Let go of the grim-faced determination and live for today.

ACTION STEP

Have you been unnecessarily censoring yourself in some way? Perhaps by dressing in a bland fashion or keeping quiet all the time or avoiding good-natured humor? Take five or ten minutes today to make your working life a little more fun, whatever that means to you.

23

You may tell yourself that you can't have nice things, because you have children or you have some bad debts or you have a medical condition or you are past a certain age. All of that may be true, but perhaps there's another way to think about the situation. Rather than tell yourself ahead of time that you can't have *a*, *b*, and *c*, or can't do *x*, *y*, and *z*, ask yourself instead what you *can* have or do. Think in terms of *can* rather than *can't*. Think of the doors as being mostly open to you rather than mostly closed.

This may sound like a small shift in perspective, but it will make a difference in your life if you can maintain this point of view over time. As you begin to think of what is possible for you rather than what is impossible, you will begin to see opportunities that you didn't notice before. You will begin to take baby steps toward your end destination rather than remaining frozen in place. The old, familiar stuck feeling will become an electric sense of possibility and becoming. The dull, low emotional states will give way to bursts of energy and enthusiasm.

As you open the doors of the heart to new possibilities, they gradually become real in the outer world as well. Change begins within your own heart. This may seem irrational or unbelievable, but shifting the inner state by deliberate acts of will can make a mediocre life into something extraordinary. When this transformation takes place, you find yourself filled with gratitude in a way that wasn't possible before.

The inner gloom gives way to an abiding sense of contentment and joy. Each year seems more amazing than the year before.

ACTION STEP

Get out a few sheets of paper and write about your ideal life for twenty-five to thirty minutes. Write about the kind of job you would like to have, the sort of house where you would like to live, the ways in which you would like to spend your time. While you are writing, cultivate the belief that everything you have in mind is completely possible for you. Maintain that attitude for the rest of the day and beyond.

24

We can technically survive without music and dance, without fine clothing and wine. We could all live in mud huts and eat bread and water. But we love ornamentation and ceremony; we long to rise above day-to-day existence and touch something celestial. We sprout angel's wings through enhancements, through finery, through poetry and song. We are the species whose essence is change; we like to manipulate reality to suit our preferences. We have been doing this since our hunter-gatherer ancestors made the first marks on the cave walls.

Each time we put pen to paper, feet to the stage, or bow to strings, we fulfill our destinies, following the leading of the muses. True abundance comes from artistry, which comes naturally to us as human beings.

We become alienated from ourselves when we refuse to accept our creative abilities, when we fail to see the plenty all around us. We have the ability to make beauty out of almost anything. The only limitations lie in our own failure to imagine. As we exercise the imagination, as we let it out of the narrow confines that we have artificially set, new worlds open to us. We can actually create new worlds with paper and pen. We can explore new worlds with our spacecraft. We can see the deepest mysteries of reality with our intellects.

We just need to set aside the gloom of self-doubt and go and make things. We are all artificers, inventors, creators, musicians, and writers. We have dexterous hands and agile minds. Amazing things happen when we put all of our heart and skill into our work, when we try with all of our might to send something wonderful into the world. We just might even surprise ourselves when we fall into the trance of creation, when we let go of ourselves and give our all to the work.

ACTION STEP

Perhaps you have lost touch with some aspect of your creative self over the years. Take some time today to write a song or a poem, to paint a picture or sketch a design. Get in touch once again with the muse inside you. Create something beautiful today.

25

We cannot do anything about the past, about the years that have already come and gone. And yet old ghosts seem to follow us. We find ourselves thinking late at night of love gone wrong, of mistakes made along the way, of plans gone awry. We turn the scenarios over again and again, asking *what if I had done things differently?* Or *I wonder what so-and-so is doing now?* In those moments, we have to ask what separates harmless reminiscence from harmful preoccupation with people and circumstances that are long gone. Ruminating on the past only makes its claim on our lives stronger. By excessively fixating on problems, we can actually magnify them and put them in the driver's seat.

It feels like steel cables tie us to decisions we made decades ago. We can lighten this sense of burden and restriction by thinking about the many freedoms that remain to us. We don't have to be the same people that we were ten or twenty years ago. We can have healthier relationships, better finances, and more satisfying work than ever before. We just have to be honest about what we want from life and go and claim it.

The biggest obstacle of all is a simple lack of clarity; we think we want one thing when we really want something else entirely. Or we disregard what we really want, because we are afraid of what people might think. We are all secretly afraid of being labeled shallow or shameless if we go for what we really want. So we play this game of managing other people's expectations, trying to be the good son or daughter, the good parent, the good spouse. There is nothing wrong with having committed relationships in our lives, but sometimes we can lose ourselves in the process of trying to do everything right.

We have to ask ourselves who we would be if we could be anyone, if there were no restrictions placed on our choices and personalities. Once we have in place a vision for an ideal life, we can then begin to see the areas where we need to make some changes. Those changes might be simple, like a wardrobe update, or major, like moving to a new job or a new city. The important thing is that we find ourselves even as we maintain our relationships.

ACTION STEP

What mistakes from your past still have a hold on you? Take a few minutes to call each preoccupation to mind, and then release each one. You might wish to say a simple affirmation, such as *I let go of the past*, each time you find yourself dwelling on events long gone.

26

Our personalities have many layers. We begin with our innermost thoughts and feelings, and, from there, we move to our physical bodies. Then we have our clothing and accessories, which are also ways of expressing our identities. The self extends to our immediate environs, to the ways that we arrange our physical spaces, our homes and offices. These choices of how to adorn or modify our bodies, of how to decorate our physical spaces, change the way that we feel and the ways other people perceive us. There is a kind of alchemy in the approach that we take toward the body and physical space; we can change the way we feel by modifying the extended self.

There are, of course, ancient arts devoted to the arrangement of space; think about *feng shui* in China or Indian *vastu* practice. And there are Western customs as well, like art deco, Shaker, or mission style. These stylings of space have emotional valences, exerting calm or sophistication, charm or elegance. If we pay attention to spaces and the emotional effects that they have on us, we can learn to manipulate our environments in favorable ways, to achieve the mental states that we would like to have.

No one ever says, *I want to feel stressed all of the time,* or *I would like to have a suboptimal day,* and yet we unconsciously allow clutter and ugliness to overtake our lives. Everything moves at such a fast pace that it can be hard to stay on top of laundry and cleaning, mail and minor repairs. We sometimes feel attached to possessions that we didn't even want to begin with. Somehow we have to learn to pause more often to set things in order, and to take conscious control of our surroundings.

Everyone probably has one area at home or work that causes trouble; it just feels unwelcoming or off-kilter. Chances are this represents some sort of blockage in life. A stack of papers could be a book or article unwritten. An untidy bathroom could signal an issue with physical appearances or self-esteem. A cluttered living room could project troubles with social interaction. As you begin to clear these spaces, you can also resolve problems in your life.

ACTION STEP

Take a look around your home or office and identify the problem areas. Then pick one area that you find to be the most distressing. Make a plan for how to improve the situation. You may be able to tackle the problem yourself, or you may need professional help from an organizer or contractor. Make both a short-term and a long-term plan to make the space feel better.

27

Making positive changes in life necessarily entails upsetting the existing order. As you pursue your dreams, the people in your life may feel alienated or resentful. To you, the pursuit of your goals will seem like a natural extension of your personality. Your friends and family, along with your spouse or significant other, may find the changes abrupt or incautious. Be prepared for people to get upset when you try to improve your life, whether the changes are major or minor.

You will undoubtedly go through periods where you feel lonely and afraid. These feelings are a sign that you are living your destiny, that you are moving into previously unexplored space. Take these feelings of hurt and use them to fuel your work. There is nothing better for an artistic or athletic pursuit than to take feelings of abandonment or isolation and turn them into some new freedom of expression. Negative feelings that have been converted into art no longer sting.

Concentrate on what you want to be born into the world. Guide your creations, little by little, into seeing the light of day. Nurture your work carefully and steadily. What now feels like a fragile thing will soon be strong enough to stand on its own. Give yourself the gift of a fully realized creation. The half-formed thoughts that you nurture today will become the work of art for tomorrow. As you give this gift to yourself, you also give it to the world.

As you go through this challenge, if you embrace it fully, you may find that it feels like your world is coming apart. It will feel like you are disassembling everything and starting all over again. This will be a painful process at times, as all change requires a measure of pain. But a new self is being born within you, and you will emerge from this process more beautiful and more resilient. You will be able to escape from the morass of inactivity and forge a brighter future for yourself.

ACTION STEP

Have you experienced some fallout in your relationships as you try to improve your life? Take a few minutes to perceive the situation from the other person's perspective. Think of a few ways to be kind and caring to the people in your life, but, at the same time, make sure that you stay on track with your goals.

28

We picture inspiration as a cartoon light bulb switching on above a creative person's head, which gives the impression that new ideas come via a sudden revelation. These epiphanies do happen, but I would venture to guess that they are the exception rather than the rule. Most of the time, inventions and discoveries come through painstaking effort over a long period of time, with lots of trial and error, just like Edison's light bulb.

The process of creation, whether artistic, scientific, or otherwise, happens in a much more messy and intuitive way than we imagine. We are driven by hunches and intuitions, which only acquire solidity and acceptance as these ephemeral things are molded into forms fit for mass consumption. At bottom, we are guided by dreams and visions, walking luminous highways crafted by the mind. We don't know where these phantasmic roads lead until we take them. It is as though the pavement appears beneath our feet only as we walk it.

The creation of anything new—a poem, a play, an article, an invention—requires faith and imagination as prerequisites. The intellect accepts the challenge posed to it by the imagination. The imagination says, *hey, here's this cool thing I dreamed*. The intellect dutifully sets to work, gamely finding the tools needed to make the cool new thing take shape. For this hand-off to take place, the imagination must first be freed to dream.

Your imagination is truly one of your greatest gifts. It lies not just behind the arts but also behind the sciences. It is as important in physics as it is in theater and ethics. The imagination allows you to see the hidden structures of nature, it allows you to put yourself in another person's position, and it allows you to see old problems in new ways. Make it your task to exercise imagination from childhood right up into old age. Imagination makes us better people, and it allows us to live in richer worlds.

ACTION STEP

Do something today to foster your imagination. Write a short story, draw a picture, or just sit somewhere in nature and daydream.

29

We all have a subconscious self that is struggling to make its way into daylight, a sort of shadow government in the recesses of our minds that can make its presence known only covertly. The subconscious self is more real, closer to our true identities than the personas that we wear for other people. Sometimes we deny it so much that we are not even sure whether or not it is real. Because we put so much effort into subduing this shadow self, this inner child or alter ego, it can only speak to us through coded messages.

We can get into touch with the inner self by paying attention to our dreams, by using artwork and music, through meditation and trance. We have to disarm the conscious mind and allow it to relax, so that the hidden self can have a little bit of free rein to operate. When the conscious mind begins to relax through deep breathing and meditation, through hypnosis or ecstatic experience, the messages from the subconscious mind can begin to slip through the censorship regime imposed by the conscious mind.

The shadow self or alter ego is generally less socially acceptable than our waking self. It may be more artistic or have a different gender or sexual identity. It may be more comfortable with sensuality and earthiness. The shadow self wants what it wants, and it will keep on trying to exert itself until its messages are heard and received. The spiritual struggle is one of tapping into the inner self and then forging a sort of peace treaty with the conscious and subconscious minds. We have to find a way to make our inner selves agree with the way that we present ourselves to the world.

As you are reading these lines, you may already have a pretty good idea of what your inner self is trying to say to you. It may want you to take up painting or drawing, it may want you to make some changes in your romantic life, or it may want you to detach from some person who is causing you emotional harm. If you feel out of touch with your inner self, there are myriad techniques for accessing the subconscious, from dream interpretation to tarot cards to hypnosis to meditation.

ACTION STEP

If you had to picture your inner self or alter ego, what would it look like? Would it be a spirit guide, a guardian angel, an inner child? Would it be male, female, or androgynous? Would it be rebellious or meek? If you had to give it a name, what would it be? Take some time to give some definition to your inner being, and then speak to it throughout the day. Give your inner self permission to come into the light more often; tell your inner self that it is safe for it to find expression in the world.

30

When we find ourselves filled with worry, concentrating only on difficulties, we are not working from a place of strength. Mired in negative thoughts, we cannot find the way to peace of mind, which can only be found by taking a step back and re-centering ourselves. An anxious mind produces quick fixes, workarounds that provide an escape from the immediate crisis but do nothing to improve the bigger picture. A calm mind can take a wider view and work to produce lasting benefits on multiple fronts.

This is where lifestyle becomes really important. It can feel like it takes a daunting investment of time to get exercise, eat properly, and practice meditation, but, over the long term, these habits lead to a completely different frame of mind. Holistic lifestyle choices make for a less reactive style of decision-making, in which the focus is less on putting out the fire of the moment and more about moving into a peaceful and harmonious existence overall. Those who put the focus on well-being will be able to move through difficulties more gracefully, taking steps toward a better life with less negativity.

Holistic well-being actually improves performance, whether we are talking about doing better at work or having stronger relationships or getting more satisfaction out of life. It just makes sense that living a healthier lifestyle leads to better outcomes overall than sacrificing well-being for the sake of material gain. Plus, when we take the time for centering, we release our constant stress and anxiety. We create a space of maneuverability in which we can find constructive solutions. Centering does not produce quick and easy results, but it will make a difference when you commit to holistic well-being over the long term.

If you amass great wealth and status but wreck your mind and body, all of that struggle will have been for naught. But if you take care of your well-being, any material success you achieve will be an added bonus.

ACTION STEP

You have now reached day thirty of this challenge and completed the first third of your journey of transformation. Take a minute to review: are you hitting your targets for diet and exercise? Are you practicing daily gratitude and visualization? Are you trying new things and seeking to improve your life? If you feel like you have fallen short in some way, do not berate yourself. Simply take note of any obstacles you have faced and make a plan to address them.

31

Live for your fans, not for your critics. Whether we are taking care of responsibilities on the job or pursuing side projects or just letting off steam on the weekends, there will always be moralistic scolds and know-it-alls. There will be trolls and bullies, opinionated observers, and not-so-neutral third parties. For every opinion voiced aloud, there will be three that we never hear. I am convinced that we worry more about what people *might* be thinking than what they actually say to our faces.

Living the boundless life means no longer predicting what other people might think and living according to *their* opinions. We will never really have access to what the crowd thinks, and, even when we do, we are not bound by their dictates. We must learn to live freely. Most of us in developed countries have come to take freedom for granted, but a truly free person is actually quite rare and far from the default setting for humanity. Freedom means following the muse wherever it might lead, even through uncertainty and difficulty. Freedom means looking for home and knowing that home may not be a geographic location or a connection to lineage and country. Freedom means finding home, and finding home is finding that self that we lost along the way, that person we would like to be but so far have failed to be. Home is being our true selves, which is far more difficult than it sounds.

Just be yourself, goes the standard advice, but *which* self? We have to learn to sort the various personas and tendencies, to find what really fits the best, what feels right in the moment. The true self does not feel confining or limiting. It does not require us to feel superior to someone else. It does not require emotional distance. The true self is an endless sort of searching, an inquiry into the best way of living in an unfolding universe.

ACTION STEP

Do you ever find yourself wondering about what judgments other people may be forming about you in their heads? Do you constantly try to second-guess their intentions and feelings? Imagine what it would be like to let go of this exhausting game of ruminating and worrying. Try to stop looking for potential issues where none exist.

32

Where I live, along the Georgia–South Carolina line, we have lots of very tall and straight pine trees, mostly white pine and longleaf pine. As a kid, I found them to be very dull trees, because they are so ubiquitous here. Now that I am a little older, I find them to be more amazing; it's actually pretty weird how tall and straight they are. They keep growing, year after year, through drought and flood and more drought. They supply the wood that we use for houses and furniture. And they do this very efficiently, sequestering carbon dioxide and spitting out oxygen.

We stand to learn a lot from the trees, the way they get everything they need while staying in one place. We people think that we have to be running around all of the time, waggling our arms and jibber-jabbering to get what we want. The trees let everything come to them, and they do things with quiet steadiness, acquiring one ring at a time. If we could be half as constant as the trees, we would accomplish great things. And we do accomplish great things; it's just that we oftentimes destroy ourselves in the process. I'm thinking about so many great actors and musicians who die too soon.

Of course, it shouldn't just be the length of life that counts but also how much love we are able to share. We're all pretty lucky to be alive; we didn't really do anything to deserve it. Most of the time, we don't realize how good we have it until something goes majorly wrong, like getting cancer or getting into a car accident. Really the only advantage we have over the trees is that we can theoretically appreciate life while we live it. Somehow we have to carry on with all of the things that we have to do while also remembering to enjoy it along the way.

We have to find a balance between making each and every day count and letting things unfold naturally. We need a mix of planning and spontaneity, discipline and play; if we go too far in either direction, we end up either getting nothing done or not having any fun. It's the simple reflections that we so easily pass over in our quests to be consequential, important people. The pine tree grows straight and tall, but its arms also sway in the wind, and its roots explore to find the water underground.

ACTION STEP

Do you feel the need to plan every single minute of the day, or are you completely spontaneous, preferring to fly by the seat of your pants? Whatever your approach to life, try doing things a little differently today. If you are an obsessive organizer, take a day off from your calendar and to-do list. If you are averse to organization, go for a few days with more regimentation, and see how that feels.

33

In the Winnie-the-Pooh books, by A.A. Milne, and in the cartoon versions, the cast of characters in the Hundred Acre Wood is anchored by personalities at two extremes. Eeyore, the stuffed donkey, perpetually holds his head low, feels sorry for himself, and has a grim interpretation of events. On the opposite end, Tigger, the bouncing tiger, always has a buoyant spirit, even when the adventures get sticky, oftentimes involving a beehive and a swarm of angry bees. Tigger bounces his way through life, while Eeyore mopes his way through his. Tigger outsmarts the bees; Eeyore believes in the pointlessness of resistance. The other characters, like Piglet and Pooh, have their ups and downs, falling somewhere in the middle. All of us fall on this spectrum, lying somewhere on the continuum between defeatist resignation and confident striving.

We all have a natural set-point, based on our life experiences and lifestyle choices, and, to some degree, our genetic background. As a result of the feedback loop between body, brain, and environment, our moods become self-reinforcing over time. An unhappy person will tend to decrease social contact and physical activity, which only deepens the negative emotional state, while a carefree person will engage with the world in a positive manner, which prolongs the good attitude. Like the flywheel on a steam engine, habit has a way of perpetuating emotional states, making them feel ingrained or even inescapable. But we live in a world of contingency and change; nothing in this world is ever immutable. Even the most stubborn personality can be moved, maybe not 180 degrees, but at least a little bit. Everyone can benefit from a little brightening of the mental landscape. We all deserve to feel a little better, whether in the context of our personal worlds or about the direction of society as a whole.

A good inner attitude will change not only how you feel but also the external circumstances of your life. You will see opportunities that you did not know were there. You will improve your relationships and feel more satisfied at work and at home. Your physical health will see benefits as well: you will go from perhaps grudgingly going to the gym every once in a while to being excited about daily physical activity. You will become more curious about the world and find wonder and beauty where you had previously ignored it. Some of these changes may have already happened for you during this challenge, but, if they haven't, take heart. Each day is a new chance to begin again, to live with more positivity and joy than the day before.

ACTION STEP

Take a few minutes to practice deep belief in yourself. Concentrate first on your body and your physical health: imagine your body getting all of the nourishment and exercise that it needs. Turn next to your working life: see yourself being fully satisfied on the job and receiving good compensation and benefits. Turn next to your emotional state: visualize yourself happy and fulfilled. Then think about your social life: picture yourself with plenty of friends that you love and good connections to your family. Finally, imagine your higher power, in whatever form you might interpret that phrase, whether it might be God or the gods or the universe itself. Picture the higher power supporting you in your endeavors, giving you everything you need for a boundless life. Repeat this exercise whenever you need a boost in your mood.

34

The standard advice to writers is to "silence the inner critic," and I think that's a good approach to life in general. Just do the work, and don't worry about the results. If you continually work for a better life, you will one day find yourself in a better place. Your willingness to at least give this challenge a shot is the first step toward a more fulfilling existence. As you make bold attempts at a new life, your confidence grows. You become more and more the person you would like to be. You venture into the unknown and begin to take calculated risks that lead you closer to your ideal life.

Risk is an inherent part of any undertaking, from writing a book to driving to work to making a podcast to baking a cake. Things can always go wrong, and they frequently do. Predictably, the inner critic will always seize upon what might go wrong rather than admitting the possibility that things could go well. The inner critic is trying to be helpful, but, if we listen to it too often, we end up paralyzed, unable to summon the energy that we need to make it to the wondrous reality that we want. And rarely is a failure complete and final; we learn from our mistakes, we grow as people, and we do better the next time around.

We tend to think that there are two binary outcomes—"failure" and "success"—which are forever distinct and opposite. But the reality is far more messy than this scenario admits. We fall upward through the projects that only halfway accomplish what we wanted from them. We take the unused portions of our old plans and recycle them. We make friends and contacts through the endeavors that we undertake. By trying, whether we succeed or fail, we find our inspiration in life.

As we light our own lives, as we find our own inspiration, we become examples for those in our lives. We look deep within and summon the courage to put our true selves out into the world. We finally put aside resentment and self-doubt and live according to our truest visions. Life then becomes a festival rather than a funeral, a celebration rather than a lament, a comedy rather than a tragedy. We expand our capacity for joy and let go of the feelings of lack and limitation. This inner struggle simultaneously represents the best hope for the world.

ACTION STEP

What do you know, in your heart of hearts, that you really need to do to find a boundless life, whatever that means for you? Chances are that you have some fear around doing whatever that is. Fear is actually a good indicator that you are on the right track; fear is your friend. Take some small step today, in spite of fear, to that thing that you have been delaying for so long.

35

If we live sedentary lives, our minds and bodies develop pathologies that can be ameliorated, if not cured, through physical activity. In the sphere of physical health, these pathologies include obesity, diabetes, and heart disease. In the sphere of mental health, sedentary lifestyles heighten anxiety and unhappiness, silent plagues that affect millions.

Physical health and mental health cannot be completely separated, as they are two sides of the same coin. Too often we think of the body as a mere support for the mind's activities, as though our physical frames were just there to move the head around, like an avatar in a video game. But the body and the mind are intrinsically bound with one another. Our bodies have neural elements from the top of our heads to the tips of our toes, and our brains, likewise, can only work with the information that we give them from our surroundings. A rich physical life leads to a rich mental life and vice versa. A life filled with new experiences and new people, novelty and surprise, will lead to a healthy mind. To put it simply, a varied and active life leads to health, and a routinized and sedentary life leads to illness.

Does this mean that every illness is caused by lifestyle factors? Well, I'm afraid not. We can't rely on wellness regimens alone. We will all need modern medicine from time to time, and it is far better to catch problems early rather than waiting for them to get worse. But having an active lifestyle pays for itself twice: first, by making life more satisfying, and second, by increasing health and well-being. Taking care of yourself does not have to be a chore. Looking and feeling good makes life easier and more fun!

ACTION STEP

The elements of this Boundless Life Challenge are making time for daily physical exercise, practicing gratitude and visualization, eating a healthy, vegetarian diet, and opening ourselves to new experiences. Which parts of the challenge are most difficult for you? Brainstorm these parts of the challenge to see how you can make them go more easily for you.

36

A single leaky water faucet can waste thousands of gallons in a year. That steady *drip, drip, drip* really adds up. If we think about our time in the same way, a small waste of time here and there easily becomes *weeks* of wasted time when stretched over a year. By the same token, a little productive use of time each day easily adds up to massive amounts of productivity. The little things lead to the big things.

As adults, we can be quite overwhelmed by all of the decisions that we have to make with our time and money. A great deal of clarity can be gained by asking, *what is the most important thing that I have to do today?* If we continually keep our minds on the most important things and tackle those priorities one step at a time—drip by drip, penny by penny, minute by minute—we will not fail to be successful. We should read success not as having a giant mansion or millions of dollars, but by how well we hold to our values in life, how well we treat others, how well we live according to our best lights.

A span of life sounds pretty long at first glance; these days people in developed nations can expect to live seventy or eighty years on average. If we believe some of the hype about new technologies and medicines, we could easily live to be over a hundred, if not longer. But all of that time doesn't mean much if we can't do the right things today. By doing good things today, we befriend our future selves, and we make the world a better place for everyone.

Thinking of time as a leaky faucet, what ways do you most frequently waste time? Try to cut that wasted time in half today. Is there something that you have been meaning to get done, but you just can't seem to find the time? Spend five minutes on the neglected task right away.

37

We see our family, friends, and coworkers all the time, but are we really connecting? Sometimes it feels like, as a society, we have forgotten how to really pay attention to anything at all. We hear but we do not listen, look but do not notice. We are so focused on getting to the next thing on the agenda that we don't attend to the person right in front of us. Or we are so entranced by technology that we forget about real life altogether. I am not at all a technophobe, but I do think that we need to pay much closer attention to the effects that our devices are having on our relationships.

We need to be more deliberate about how we connect with those around us, whether they be friends or neighbors, clients or customers. We receive clues all the time about what matters to our loved ones, but so often we miss the feedback that they are giving us. I don't think that most people are particularly selfish, just preoccupied. It takes a good deal of effort to pry ourselves away from distraction, to put aside stress and worries and really listen deeply. The work of deep attention can be healing, both for ourselves and for the people in our lives.

As we foster true connection with others, we also get in touch with our true selves. When we go off script in conversation, letting things unfold naturally, we put ourselves into a more vulnerable position. We let down the armor that we so frequently wear, and we really encounter the other person. We risk getting to know ourselves better as we see ourselves reflected through the eyes of our partners. We set aside the status quo situation of distraction and enter into a space of true relationship. On some level, we really fear intimacy with other people, and yet it is also what we deeply crave.

As individuals, we don't really have all of the pieces to the puzzle. The answers to our questions can be found only through relationship. You can have the boundless life that you want only when you let go of your defenses and learn to trust once again in other people. Then you can begin to build truly healthy and effective relationships that take you to the place of abundance where you want to be. You can begin this process by listening, both to your own heart and to the messages coming to you from others. The journey to boundless life occurs in this space of dialogue between the inner self and these sacred others.

ACTION STEP

Today, practice deep listening to whoever comes into your life, whether that might be a spouse or romantic partner, a student or colleague, a client or customer. While you are in the conversation, strive to stay fully engaged with the other person. After the conversation is over, take a minute to write some notes. What did that person convey to you? What follow-up questions do you need to ask?

38

Bicyclists can control only a few factors while riding a bike: the force that they put into the pedals, the choice of gears, and the cadence of pedaling. Higher rotations per minute are more efficient; the circulatory system, the muscle fibers, and the machine of the bike itself coordinate to produce maximum output (i.e., distance). Getting into those higher RPMs requires a lot of training, but, once those higher levels have been reached, more work can be done with less exertion.

When we go out cycling, we want to turn the pedals over faster, move into higher gears, and exert more pressure. This translates into distance and speed. The very same factors are at work for a kid tooling around the block and an elite athlete in training. The level of training varies, but the basic principles do not. We can all improve our cycling through practice and coaching, but we should also try to have fun, like kids going down the biggest hill in the neighborhood.

The lessons that apply in cycling pertain to all aspects of life. We become more adept at our jobs as we increase throughput in a smaller amount of time. We have to strive to do the same amount of work in twenty hours that once took forty hours, without decreasing quality. That last bit is pretty important: form is key, both in cycling and in ordinary life.

As we gain more skills on the job, the tasks that once seemed daunting come to seem second nature. We accomplish more work without seeming flustered. Even the busy hours and seasons roll over us like water off a duck's back. We stop fixating on the pain and the inertia and simply do the work that needs to be done. We no longer get bogged down in the details, and time flows smoothly. Everything proceeds with maximum efficiency.

ACTION STEP

Are you putting enough energy into your work, or are you stuck in a low gear? Try doing everything in an efficient manner today, working as quickly as possible without getting sloppy. See how much work you can plough through, which will then leave more time for self-care or creative pursuits.

39

Many years ago, I stumbled across a book called *Blind Courage*, by Bill Irwin, who was the first blind person to hike the Appalachian Trail. In the book, he recounts the thousands of times that he fell on the more than 2,000-mile journey, continually bashing his knees and breaking his ribs. His guide dog, Orient, became so adept at hiking that he learned to read the white blazes marking the trail. Another important aspect of the story is that Bill Irwin also overcame alcoholism in addition to learning to adapt to blindness resulting from a rare disease.

Bill Irwin died in 2014 at the age of seventy-three, but he and his dog—the pair were known as the "Orient Express"—remain an inspiration to many. They remind us that we can triumph over any disability or tragedy, even the forces of nature. With the help of our friends—be they human or nonhuman—we can do anything. We need force of will, commitment, and courage, but the future lies open to us, regardless of injury, addiction, poverty, or any other factor. All we have to do is stop feeling sorry for ourselves, stop dwelling on the past, and find something sufficiently inspiring to do with our lives.

We don't all have to hike from Georgia to Maine, but we do have our own struggles and our own dreams. We eventually are able to look upon the mistakes we have made, whether they might be failed relationships, career mishaps, health issues, or struggles with addiction, as lessons learned rather than full-stop disasters. We learn to orient ourselves along the journey of life, overcoming our blindness by getting in touch with our guidance systems. We look to our elders, to our spiritual teachers, to our companion animals, and to the divinity within. We make our way, one faltering step at a time, toward the goal of a fulfilling life.

All of us go through periods of feeling inspired and other periods where we do not know day from night. We can collapse sometimes into self-pity and resignation. But there is always the opportunity to start over again. You don't have to be limited by the events that happened in the past. You can make the move from being a victim of circumstance to being the author of your own destiny. That takes a little bit of Bill Irwin's blind courage.

ACTION STEP

What struggles emerged in your past that prevented you from moving forward in life? Make a quick mental list or write them down on paper. As you go down the list, make a commitment to yourself that you will no longer be bound by the past. For each item on the list, think of a workaround or strategy to address each limitation that you face.

40

Archimedes is said to have taken a bath in a full tub and noticed that his body displaced some of the water, which led to the conclusion that the volume of his body could be accurately measured by taking note of the volume of the water displaced. He shouted "Eureka!," which means "I have found it!," while running naked through the streets of Syracuse, Sicily.

Is the story real, or is it just another nice story, like Ben Franklin and his key tied to a kite string? Does it matter if the story is real? Certainly these moments of discovery do happen. But they happen to people who are plugged into their communities, who are part of an active program of research. We could say that such discoveries come about as part of the larger situation within communities of inquiry devoted to a common search. Philosopher of science Thomas Kuhn describes this process in his classic work, *The Structure of Scientific Revolutions*.

The lone genius working in isolation really amounts to a single node in a larger network, usually one spanning many countries and time periods. Such an image can be humbling, for it means that no single inquirer really has the answer and that the big problems span the centuries and not just the years. But it can also be empowering, because it means that all we have to do is contribute to the conversation rather than revolutionizing it. Even if we seem to be fundamentally changing the way people view the world, such shifts appear so dramatic only in hindsight. Upon closer inspection, the historian, armchair or credentialed, will find a series of smaller steps that led to the revolutionary change.

Imagine for a second *not needing* profound epiphanies; imagine achieving your goals by just showing up every day and doing mundane work. Kuhn calls this "normal science," the regular effort of showing up at the lab; most of us just call it the daily grind. Even if we might whine about the quotidian nature of our professions, we have to remember that there is some magic sprinkled in there, or maybe it's a little bit of Archimedes' bathwater. Good things come to those who accrue smaller efforts, day by day.

ACTION STEP

Do you find yourself waiting for inspiration before beginning work on your projects? Today, work on one of your stalled endeavors for half an hour, regardless of whether or not you feel inspired. See if you do not feel better at the end of the half hour than you did at the beginning.

41

Sometimes we are afraid to act, because we keep asking ourselves what might go wrong if we try something new. This fear of the unknown leads to stagnation in life. It can be easy to get caught in the *what if?* scenarios, which are usually reserved for bad outcomes. No plan is so foolproof that there isn't something that could go wrong, but focusing on the negatives only leads to paralysis.

To break this pattern of fear and debilitation, we have to approach things more experimentally. We have to be willing to say to ourselves, *let me just try this and see what happens.* It takes courage to try something new, whether it's learning to speak French, taking up a new sport, or going on a blind date. There will be awkward moments, and we will definitely face disappointments, but the bold adventure is a thousand times better than not trying at all.

Nothing ventured, nothing gained, goes the old cliché. I think it actually goes a little deeper than that. We secretly know that, in each new undertaking, it is not just capital and time that we risk. What we risk is nothing less than our own self-definitions. We are putting *ourselves* on the line. We are risking becoming someone else, someone different. And that is a lot more risky than just being out fifty bucks or wasting a few hours.

The way you live your life has a way of seeping into your identity. That's why it's important to choose consciously how you spend your time and the company that you keep. What would you like to spend more time doing? What would you like to do less often? Luckily, you have the power to be an agent of change. You can become whoever you want.

ACTION STEP

Have you been held back in life by *what if* scenarios? Name one time in the last year that you were held back by imagining how things might have gone awry. Can you revisit your plans with a greater sense of possibility? Take one baby step today to move closer to your goal.

42

When big changes come into our lives, it can feel like the end of the world, like everything familiar is slipping away. But no change is ever really the end of the world; it is really just the end to this particular iteration, this particular aspect of life. We may move to a new city or accept a new job. We may lose friends and gain new ones. We may decide to have kids or decide not to have kids. The possibilities are endless, really. The flow of the story keeps on going, but with different characters and settings.

We find change jarring and unsettling because we trick ourselves into believing in the permanence of temporary things. Once we let go of the illusion that things will always remain the same, we see change everywhere, all around us. And when we clue into the reality of cease-less change, we also begin to see opportunities where we previously believed there were none. We also see that the situations that we find so upsetting will soon be at an end.

When we see change as the basic nature of reality, we also recognize that we have a great deal of power to affect the outcome of events. Now is just as good a time as any to get into shape, to get organized, to take charge of our relationships and careers. The world is chaotic, yes, but that very same randomness is what makes the world responsive to our efforts. The universe has no plans but the ones that we supply. The universe doesn't really care if we are happy and successful, but, by the same token, it isn't out to get us, either.

As soon as you call forth order into your life, as soon as you insist on things being a certain way, circumstances begin to align in that manner. All you have to do is form a certain vision of how you want your life to look and then take steps to make that vision a reality. You will very soon begin to find allies who can help you make it to the goal. You find resources that you had not previously noticed. Is this magic? Only the magic of conscious choice, the power of thought to bring structure into random events.

ACTION STEP

Say to yourself, *someone has to be happy and successful; it might as well be me. Someone has to have good and fulfilling relationships; it might as well be me. Someone has to be talented and attractive; it might as well be me.* Keep going along with this line of thought for a few minutes. For each positive outcome you can imagine, say to yourself, *it might as well be me.*

43

No one can really tell us *how* to be happy in life, because happiness is unique to each individual. We don't know how to make our loved ones happy, and sometimes we don't even know how to make ourselves happy. Our schemes for finding happiness often end in failure, because we fail to appreciate the mysterious nature of it all. The question of happiness is usually something we confront only when something major happens, whether it be a good or not-so-good thing.

If we are to have any hope of finding happiness, we have to go through a self-interrogation. We can look back over the years and find the times when we felt most at ease, most joyful and serene. Then, rather than just wax nostalgic, we can ask why things were working well at that particular time. We can also look back over the dark and gloomy times and ask why they were so dark and gloomy. Each time we analyze our own stories, we get a little better at understanding why things went the way they did. We come a little closer to self-understanding, which is the one prerequisite for happiness.

Self-understanding is not easy. We can get a little bit of it by going to a therapist or by writing in a journal or by talking with close friends and intimate companions. Still, we can miss things for years and even decades. Sometimes we aren't ready to hear hard truths about ourselves. But the more we open ourselves to insight, the greater the chance that we will have the clarity to do the emotional work that we need to do to find happiness.

We have to be skeptical of the stories we tell ourselves. Maybe I'm not as empathetic as I think I am, or maybe I'm really not a good listener. Maybe I don't really like baseball, and I only pretended to like it to please Uncle Jimmy or whoever. We have to sort our own motivations and behaviors, to separate the true from the false. This is very difficult, because we have so much propaganda wrapped up in our psyches. We have the family story, the passed-down mythologies and rationalizations. We have the stories we tell ourselves, which tend to be ego inflating. And then everyone in our lives has their own form of propaganda, so that it can be very hard to just live in reality.

Meditation can help us to gain some clarity, but it can also be a form of escape. We have to ask ourselves how our spiritual practices fit into the stories we tell ourselves. Am I meditating so that other people will think that I'm a swell guy? Am I seeking from God or Enlightenment what I did not get in childhood? No one ever comes to these practices with perfectly pure intentions; even Jesus and the Buddha had to go through ordeals and temptations. You just need to get familiar with your own stories and make sure that you are being honest with yourself.

ACTION STEP

Ask yourself what forms of propaganda are at work in your own life. You can do this by writing in a journal or by just mentally examining your life. Specifically, what do you believe about yourself that you suspect may not be true? What stories were passed down in your family that were distorted in order to frame one person as a hero and another person as a monster? What stories do you tell yourself with regard to your relationships? Do you have a tendency to view yourself as a martyr or a hero? Do you paint your spouse or significant other in an unflattering light? How can you correct these stories so that they bear a closer resemblance to the truth?

44

I ran cross country for two years in high school. I was a solidly middle- to back-of-the-pack runner, having had very little experience with sports up until that point. I don't do ball sports at all; when I throw a ball, it is just as likely to go sideways or backward as it is to go where I want it to go. I still think I got a lot out of the experience of running cross country, especially since I didn't have to throw or catch. Coach Eddie and Coach Dave would tell us to "work the hills," the idea being that anyone can run quickly down hills, so running quickly uphill leads to a competitive advantage. There were moments when I actually enjoyed running uphill and racking up miles, despite all of the knee pain and shin splints.

I still run as a way of staying in shape, and I'm still not very fast. But I do like pushing myself, doing a longer race every now and then, going out on the roads and trails. Occasionally, I'll even do some hill repeats and other drills. When I'm doing hill repeats, my lungs feel like they are going to explode out of my chest, and I suck in the dust that comes from my shoes. My shirt gets drenched in sweat. I'm still not going to be in first place or even win my age group, but I know that I have tried my hardest and pushed past my own limits. What really counts is how we measure up to the goals that we set for ourselves, not whether or not we qualify as elite athletes.

Our culture needs more everyday athleticism. We have plenty of superstars, and that's all well and good, but we need more attention given to sports for regular people. And I don't mean just going through the motions of keeping fit, but actually getting out there and having fun with it. We have to get rid of the notion that sports are reserved for an elite few. Physical activity is not just for LeBron James, Usain Bolt, Katie Ledecky, and Kate McIlroy, or any of the other luminaries in various sports that you see on your TV screen. Sports can simply be about testing ourselves and having a good time.

Of course the competitive element is always there. It can be disappointing to train for an event for months, only to perform worse than expected or have the race get rained out. It can be demoralizing to be passed in a race by someone you think you should be able to beat or to get injured or have equipment fail. But the real victory lies in just getting out there. The person who comes in last on race day is still ahead of the thousands of people just lying on the couch eating Cheetos. And the journey from couch to 5K or from 5K to marathon is not as long as you might think.

ACTION STEP

Go online and find any type of race (running, swimming, biking, etc.) that you would like to do. Go ahead and sign up for it, making sure to leave enough time for training. Download a training schedule or make one yourself, and go ahead and do that first workout.

45

I went to the Shaky Knees music festival in Atlanta with my wife, Jessica, and our friend, Ashley, a couple of years ago. The bands were pretty good, and we had some Indian food downtown. Then we ordered a Lyft driver to take us back to Ashley's apartment, and that was when things started to go a little sideways.

The driver, Lee, explained that he had a job in the funeral industry and that he was saving money to start a nudist colony in the Pacific Northwest. "It's going to be called Bare Necessities, get it?" he laughed. I was sitting in the front seat, and I could tell there was something off about Lee, the sort of intense look in his eyes. If I had to guess, I'd say he was on speed or acid. Driving in Atlanta is crazy on a good day, but Lee was taking it to a new level, darting in and out of traffic and making last-second left turns. On the plus side, we made a thirty-minute drive in ten minutes with our lives intact.

We joke about it from time to time, but it is probably true that one of us or all of us could have died, either by traffic accident or serial killer. But isn't that also true on any random weekday? We could all get killed by funeral home Lee, but then we could just as easily get killed while walking down the sidewalk. It is good to be cautious, but not so cautious that it becomes impossible to go places and do things. So, by all means, read the reviews before riding but also talk to strangers and get into weird situations.

A completely safe life is also a completely dull life. Don't get me wrong: condoms are a good means of preventing sexually transmitted infections, and seat belts and airbags are good ideas. You don't have to go skydiving if you don't want to, and parkour on top of a forty-story building is a bad idea. Don't eat shrimp if you have a shellfish allergy. But also don't miss a good experience because something bad might happen.

ACTION STEP

Congratulations on making it halfway through this challenge! You have already made some steps toward pushing back against fear and creating a better life for yourself. Just as a reminder, this challenge involves doing the gratitude exercise and the visualization exercise every day (see "Exercising Gratitude" and "Seeing the Destination" in Part 1). The other parts of the challenge are eating a healthy diet and exercising every day. The last part of the challenge (and the most intangible part) is to try new things and expand your sense of possibility. Which parts of the challenge have you found to be the most difficult so far? How can you push through your limitations for the remaining forty-five days?

46

"Weird Al" Yankovic has made an entire career for himself out of parodying pop songs. Jenna Marbles, of *YouTube* fame, makes a living by playing dress-up with her dogs and trying Internet beauty tips. These examples show that you don't have to be good at everything to be successful; you just have to find a niche and stick with it.

I don't know if Al or Jenna really planned to be quite as successful as they are. They just had this unique ability and ran with it. That sort of thing can't be planned, necessarily. I think that what is amazing about these performers is that they didn't censor themselves or try to fit into a mold of what success should look like. I also admire their wackiness and sense of humor; it is nice to have a little bit of relief from the worries and stress of life.

Sometimes we make things too hard for ourselves by trying to achieve some idea of success that is really someone else's shtick. We have to just do what we do well. When we follow our individual paths, one thing leads to another. We don't have to scramble so much to find work. Things flow a little more naturally, and the ideas just come. All we have to do is keep going, keep creating, keep just being our same dorky selves.

When we self-censor, trying to be cool or hip or whatever, it ends up being kind of artificial. There is no predicting what other people will like; we never know when the lightning will strike. It's better to just follow the work wherever it leads. The inner aspect of the work is to try to stay true to ourselves. The outer aspect of the work is to do the best job that we possibly can. After we have done the work, the rest is out of our hands.

ACTION STEP

Have you been holding back on one of your ideas because you thought it was too strange or dorky? Go ahead and give your weird idea a chance. Work on your plan for a few minutes today.

47

The three common limiting factors of time, space, and money aren't really separate; they feed into one another. If you find yourself lacking one of these resources, devote energy to one of the others instead. For example, if you find yourself eating ramen noodles and peanut butter because your bank account is down to eight dollars, it may be true that you don't have money to invest in your dreams; but you may have a couple of hours that you could spend writing that short story or learning to ice skate or pursuing whatever your dream might be.

Maybe your home isn't as spacious as you would like it to be, but you could go to a public park to do yoga or walk your dog or whatever makes you feel healthy and energetic. Or maybe your junky old computer doesn't run well and needs replacing. You don't have the money yet to replace it, but you could spend some time researching exactly the right model that will suit your needs. Spending time on a project is just as much of an investment as spending money, so doing this kind of productive research does move you closer to your goals.

As you begin to use the resources that you do have, other resources will begin to open to you. As you exercise your skills and abilities, you find ways to work in ways that feed you, emotionally and spiritually, while also earning money that you will need for self-advancement. One success leads to another, and you get your own momentum going, slowly but steadily. Each daily effort brings new opportunities.

ACTION STEP

Of the three limiting factors of time, space, and money, which one gives you the biggest headaches? Find some way to use your other resources to compensate for the perceived lack.

48

Creativity is the cup that runs over: we can drink from it again and again, and yet it replenishes itself. Inspiration is like the tides, coming and going each day, bringing the waves crashing into the beach. These metaphorical ways of speaking acknowledge that we can never really run out of ideas: the more we express ourselves through writing or music, poetry or dance, the more avenues of expression lie open to us. It is the same way with any sort of physical activity: the more we exhaust ourselves, the more energy we seem to have.

We can even fight against the aging of our minds and bodies by choosing to use the faculties that we have. As we exercise our minds, our wits remain sharp. As we exercise our bodies, they age more slowly and gracefully. As we nourish ourselves in mind, body, and spirit, we actually grow stronger with each passing year. We can hold onto the powers that we have by continually using them. And if we should lose some ability, we can compensate for that loss by staunchly defending what remains to us. We can make our lives into works of art, and this is true at any stage of life, in any physical or mental condition.

We will all have one problem or another with aging and ill health, but our mindset with regard to these events makes all the difference. We can choose to resign ourselves and go along with decline, or we can exert ourselves and improve the outlook. The fates don't look down on us from the heavens; they reside in our hearts. Our destinies are not handed to us; we consciously choose them.

If you don't like what you see in your future, do something about it. Look for the adventures that speak to you. Learn the skills that you most desire. Find the company that you want to keep. Good seasons and bad seasons will come and go, but, if you retain your inner resolve, you will preserve a sense of possibility.

ACTION STEP

What aspects of your future do you find the most daunting? Is it the prospect of health problems or financial issues or a dull routine? Make a plan today to address your concerns.

49

Cynicism masquerades as a realistic worldview based on hard-won struggle, but it is really just another defense mechanism. If I adopt a cynical view toward politics, it means that I don't have to get involved. If I am cynical about my workplace, it means I can justify not giving my full effort. Letting go of the cynicism means that I have to face my own lackluster performance, and that can be frightening. It is much easier to blame *the system* or *the company* rather than take my share of the blame.

We can get more out of life through engagement with meaningful projects than we can get from commenting from the sidelines. If we have time to complain, then we have time to do something about it. Instead of getting angry, we can take the time to organize and make phone calls, to try new ideas and network with others. This constructive behavior stands a much better chance of actually changing things than does mere complaining.

Instead of griping about how digital devices are ruining our social interactions, we can participate in Screen-Free Week or National Novel Writing Month. Instead of whining about how fast food companies make our diets terrible, we can plant gardens and cook at home more often. Instead of just yelling at the television news, we can write letters to the editor or join advocacy organizations.

Doing something is a powerful antidote to cynicism, which thrives on lethargy. When we take action, no matter how small that action might be, we can let go of poisonous negativity and begin to feel a little better about our shared world. We make our communities better not only for ourselves but also for all of those who are looking to us for inspiration. The fact is that other people are looking to us for guidance, and we should try to be the best examples that we can be, as positive and proactive as possible.

ACTION STEP

In what small way could you make the world a better place? Take thirty minutes today to engage with the world, to do something constructive to work for change.

50

No one just *has time* to work on a creative project or get into shape or excel in a career. As the title of Meredith Atwood's podcast suggests, we all have *the same 24 hours*. Fortunes are made not based on extravagant efforts every now and again but by what we do on an average Tuesday afternoon. It's the daily efforts that make the difference between a dream half-realized and a dream fulfilled.

If we wait around until we have the time, we will be waiting forever. We don't have time; we make time. We have to go ahead and do the things that are most important to us, and the time has to be now. Otherwise, we just play the game of endless deferral, kicking the can down the road toward an ever-receding horizon. If something is worth doing, it is worth doing today.

To have a boundless life, a life that is truly abundant and worthwhile, we have to think of our time as limited and valuable. We have to think of time as a finite resource and not an infinite one. Everything ends, including life, so we have to appreciate it as much as possible. One of the ways of truly appreciating life and expressing our gratitude is to make each day and hour as excellent as we possibly can.

I suppose it can feel like a lot of pressure to make every moment count, but it is much better than the alternative of taking everything for granted and living passively. When we accept our own mortality and simultaneously value the beauty in life, we naturally want our lives to express the highest vision that we can conceive in our minds.

ACTION STEP

How can you make every single moment count on this average day? Try setting aside listless distraction and concentrating fully on the task at hand, whether it is doing something for work or taking a stroll outside. Using this method, you can actually work more slowly while getting more done. A one-pointed mind is more efficient than a mind that darts to and fro. Concentration leads to fewer mistakes and a better final product.

51

If you find yourself getting down in the dumps, either because of a bad day at work or a more long-term problem, it can be helpful to look for the little things that brighten your day. Maybe you like to visit record stores or have a certain type of herbal tea that you really like. Maybe you enjoy keeping in touch with a good friend or relative. Or perhaps you take solace in an imaginary world through literature. Maybe you like to play chess or do sudoku.

Our reasons for living do not have to be grand and heroic. We can live for the little things: small connections with the world are enough. We don't always need Purpose with a capital *P*: little purposes tend to keep things on the right track. The little purposes also tend to be much more forgiving: they don't demand total allegiance. They speak to our hearts, but not in an overarching way, so as to ask all of our time and attention.

When we look back on the seasons of our lives, we might associate a particular time in life with the music that we loved at the time, the food we cooked, the places we frequented. All too often we think of these associations as the background to our efforts, when really the whole of life is equally important. What we consider to be the background or subtext of life today we might consider to be of central importance five years from now or a decade from now.

These moments can sometimes surprise us with their timing and depth. A chance conversation can become a life-altering event. A few words from a song can be lifesaving. A connection to an animal or a landscape or a city can restore the will to live. These touchstones, or what Carl Jung called synchronicities, are life's way of hitting the reset button.

ACTION STEP

What little things make your life more enjoyable? Try to think of non-addictive activities and interests that make you want to get out of bed in the morning. Make a list of five things for starters and try to do at least one of them today.

52

Sometimes we go into deprivation mode as a means of coping with stress. Someone struggling with finances might reason, *Well, I have a lot of bills to pay, let me just wear used clothing and eat rice and beans until I have zero debt.* Or a student at finals time might say, *I have a lot of studying to do, so I just won't sleep until my exams.* Or a person struggling with weight control might say, *I will eat only 1,000 calories a day until I am down to my goal weight.*

The foremost problem with deprivation mode is that it doesn't work. We are all human beings, and we need to eat, sleep, and be reasonably comfortable. Any extreme habit that threatens our basic survival instincts will not be likely to succeed. The second problem is that deprivation mode often flips into its opposite: we bounce back and forth between austerity and self-indulgence pretty easily.

Moderation is a pretty good alternative to deprivation, and it has been recommended at least since Aristotle and the Buddha. But for some reason, moderation just isn't as popular as a concept. We find the extremes to be so much more titillating. We love superlatives: the world's skinniest man, the world's most difficult climb, the world's biggest corn maze. Even the gross ones get a lot of attention: the world's longest fingernails and others I don't care to mention.

Chipping away at problems one day at a time is much more effective than pursuing programs of austerity. Moderation doesn't get a lot of press, and it won't necessarily lead to superlatives. But it will lead to a more balanced and sane way of life. As we begin to drop our addiction to superlatives and extremism, we make way for simple, everyday abundance. We pursue self-discipline because it makes us happy, not because we have to punish ourselves.

ACTION STEP

Have you gone into deprivation mode in the past? What triggered your deprivation response? Most likely this issue represents one of your primary struggles in life. Could you tackle the same problem in a less extreme but still effectual way? If so, how?

53

Mishaps will occur in life, some of them major and some minor. Setbacks will happen, whether we want them or not. Things don't always go smoothly, at work or at home. While we may not be able to control every eventuality, we can control our responses to the misadventures that inevitably arise. We can respond calmly, taking things one step at a time, performing the routine work that needs to be done.

In fact, we can take comfort in routine when things are going south in some way. Even if we can't concentrate on serious intellectual work or tackle a new creative challenge, we can pretty much always match pairs of socks or make sure that the recycling gets taken to the road. These little chores don't mean very much in the grand scheme of things, but they are a sort of anchor in difficult times. They provide a sense of normalcy and grounding in times of grief or disturbance.

Routines give us a sense of safety and comfort; it is sometimes nice to know exactly what you will be doing at a certain time of day. This is especially true during times of distress. Despite all of the uncertainty in the world, it is nice to know that some things remain the same. Having a few everyday rituals can restore a sense of reliability and comfort to life. These little habits brighten our days and bring joy to life.

Meera Lester wrote *Rituals for Life*, an entire book of little daily rituals that we can use to bring comfort and meaning to life. She writes, "We perform rituals for an audience even if that audience is only ourselves. Rituals inspire dreams, spark creative vision, suggest new paths, and offer healing. They help us explore new places within ourselves and others." These practices can be as simple as having a cup of tea or as elaborate as ceremonial magic; regardless, they give us a sense of place and empowerment.

ACTION STEP

Do you have a comforting ritual in your life that helps you to preserve your sanity in times of disruption? Be sure to make time for that ritual today.

54

When we try to be more productive, either in creative pursuits or at work or in the gym, it can feel like squeezing blood from a stone. We all have so much happening in our lives that it feels impossible to keep going. Things get easier when we realize that our abundance does not come from the ego, or what I call the small mind. Our abundance comes from the universal self or the mind of the universe. When we tap into this big mind, things flow much more smoothly. Inspiration is actually all around us. We don't create it; we just gain access to it. All that is required for inspiration is an open mind and a calm heart.

As soon as I begin to settle into a calm and quiet frame of mind, the resources appear to do what needs to be done. The obstacles that I encounter while going on a trail run or a long bike ride are largely of my own making; centering myself gets rid of the inner complaints. When I find myself not knowing what to do about a situation at work, I just calm my mind. Then the action steps are given to me automatically. If I am having trouble with a particular relationship, I go into my calm space to discover how to set things right. The words that I need to say or the actions I need to take appear in my mind's eye, like a set of instructions.

This sounds quite magical, but it is an everyday sort of magic. We function better when we are not hopped up with stress and anxiety. When we attune ourselves with our bodies and the surrounding environment, calmly and deliberately, solutions just appear. The mind is not a property just of the gray matter between our ears; it exists in confluence with the right ordering of our interactions with things and other people. When the mind is properly untangled from its self-caused knots, it functions beautifully.

We don't really lack anything we need for happiness in life. We just have to patiently and persistently become aware of the resources available to us and then put those resources to work to solve the problems that arise. Even the most dire situation can be improved by opening the inner space and patiently waiting for inspiration. Then, when the ideas arrive, we have to immediately act on them to the best of our ability.

ACTION STEP

Think of a small or large situation in your life that is currently bothering you. Set an intention to solve this problem, and then spend ten to twenty minutes in silent meditation. See if any insight arises at the end of the period of silence. Then immediately take action on the inspiration given to you.

55

What if you could avoid stroke, heart disease, or diabetes? What if you could live ten years longer? If you already have serious medical problems or have had extensive surgeries, what if you could speed recovery and avoid the worst effects of the conditions you already have? Diet and exercise are more potent remedies than most prescription medications, and yet most people don't really take advantage of these natural ways to stay healthy.

This is largely because our healthcare system, in the United States at least and to some extent in other countries, is geared toward fixing things once they go wrong rather than focusing on prevention. There is also a technological bias in medicine, toward pills, procedures, and devices instead of holistic health. Some of this has to do with the financial incentive for the healthcare industry to order lots of tests, operations, and medications rather than supporting inexpensive, early interventions.

There is also the confusion factor, with so many vitamins and supplements, gadgets and regimens on offer that supposedly lead to quick weight loss or six-pack abs. A rule of thumb is that something that promises quick and easy solutions probably does not work as advertised. That's why I have designed this challenge for maximum simplicity and impact (which is not the same as being quick and easy). You really only need to remember a few things: exercise an hour a day, eat a healthy diet, practice gratitude and visualization, and keep life fun and interesting.

The rest is just details. For example, I recommend cross-training rather than doing the same sport day after day. The ninety-day bit is purposely designed as an on-ramp for more lasting change. If you can keep this routine for ninety days, you can keep it for a year. If you can keep it for a year, you can continue for a decade or a lifetime.

ACTION STEP

Have you tried quick-fix health solutions before? How did the experience go for you? What mental blocks do you need to surrender in order to experience long-lasting improvements in health and well-being? Write a page or two about wellness efforts that have not gone well for you in the past and what you are now doing differently.

56

Gentleness, as a frame of mind and as a spiritual practice, deserves to be explored in much greater detail. Perhaps because of the masculine bias of Western culture, we have a tendency to get too aggressive and be too hard on ourselves and others in both our careers and our home lives. I think one of the reasons that yoga has become so popular in the West is that it emphasizes being gentle with our bodies, being careful not to push them too far.

We can take gentleness as a practice into all areas of our lives. In our thoughts and emotional lives, we can be more free and easy with ourselves, avoiding harsh castigation and blame. We can be more gentle with our colleagues, with our spouses and children. We can practice gentleness with our companion animals and with the natural world. And we can actually be just as effective if not more effective while practicing gentleness, because we avoid overtaxing our minds and bodies.

Gentleness influences communication, thinking, and behavior. It softens nearly everything about life. It seeps into the interstices of our relationships, making things proceed more naturally. We can practice gentleness without lowering standards, without compromising on our goals, without surrendering any agency. Gentleness might change *how* we go about pursuing our goals, but it does not mean that we have to relinquish them.

Gentleness and kindness naturally go together. If a thought directed toward yourself or others is not gentle and kind, let it go. If you accidentally behave in a way that is not gentle and kind, try to make amends in some way. Speaking and acting with gentleness actually requires great skill and is much more difficult than simply barging ahead in a brusque, obtrusive manner.

ACTION STEP

Practice the gentleness test today. For every thought that arises, see if it is both kind and gentle. If it is not kind and gentle, let it go. This test can be employed with words spoken aloud or uttered in private, with actions taken in public or performed in a solitary fashion.

57

Think of ideas as little creatures who want to be born into the world. These ideas are friendly but quite shy; they come to those who have a decent shot at bringing them into our world. Having an idea is kind of like petting a newborn puppy or kitten. But because ideas are somewhat reclusive, they will flee if they are not handled properly. They need to be socialized if they are to stay in the material world, and this happens through a lot of nurturing.

Suppose you have an idea for an epic adventure you'd like to take or a mind-blowing novel you'd like to write or a birthday bash you would like to throw. Here's the thing: if you don't take action, that idea will just go away, and someone else will seem like they're having your adventure, writing your novel, throwing your party. If you take the opposite course and begin to nurture that idea and plan for it through a long gestation period, the day will come when the idea becomes reality, when that little creature comes into being.

Socrates, in a dialogue called the *Symposium*, compares the philosopher to a midwife. He may have gotten the idea from his mother, Phaenarete, who is said to have been a midwife. Socrates said that we all love beauty, and, being quite smitten with it, we want to possess beauty eternally. But, of course, we are mortal, so we can't possess anything eternally. The next best thing, he says, is procreation, which could be literally giving birth to children but could also refer to other acts of creation, like writing beautiful songs, plays, and stories.

You will not live forever, but there is the chance that your creations will outlive you. Even if your words and deeds are entirely forgotten, it is possible that you will inspire someone else, creating a chain reaction that cascades through the generations. Through creation of any sort—athletic, literary, biological, aesthetic, etc.—you can get just the slightest bit of transcendence over the ravages of time. Your powers are quite human and worldly, but, as it turns out, those normal powers are pretty amazing. You experience the power of being human every time you watch a play or an athletic competition, every time you are inspired by an amazing artist or musician.

ACTION STEP

Do you have a shy, reclusive idea that has been hovering on the edges of your consciousness for months or years? Take some time today to bring your idea closer to completion. Don't get too caught up in perfectionism: just surrender yourself to the inspiration.

58

When we get into tight spots in life, those situations of stress that lead to feeling overwhelmed, it can be easy to lash out at the people around us, even those who are close to us, who are in the best position to be able to help. People who are drowning will often flail around, putting even their rescuers in danger. When we get down into the difficult places in life, we have to keep in mind our own tendency to behave irrationally. We also need to remember that our loved ones may sometimes behave in ways that don't make sense. The path forward lies in avoiding a panicked state of mind and practicing forgiveness for actions taken under duress.

You may be going through a crisis at the moment, or maybe someone close to you is having a tough time. As we go through the seasons of life, we experience various types of dislocation and change, from moving to getting married to having a child to getting divorced—major events will happen. We all have times when we will need a strong network of support, and sometimes we will be in a position to offer support. All of us can be emotional wrecks at one time or another, but thankfully we are not all a mess at the same time.

When we give support to someone who is going through difficulty, we know that one day we will need help from others. When we receive support, we know that the time will come when we can lend a helping hand. Yet reciprocity is not a tit-for-tat game of compensation: the summons to care for someone could come at any time. Sometimes we can aid those in our immediate circle, but we may also be called to help those who are far removed by geography, ethnicity, or social class. At the end of the day, we all belong to one family. Care and concern have a way of returning to us unexpectedly.

Blockages in life can arise when we have trouble either receiving help or giving help; these two difficulties are intrinsically related. We can only come to properly care for other people when we learn to love ourselves and take care of ourselves. Our relationships tend to express what we have inside. As we learn to accept ourselves, we can have greater intimacy with friends and romantic partners. If we have a skewed self-understanding or an inability to practice self-love, our relationships with others will also suffer.

ACTION STEP

What facets of your personality or of your embodiment do you have the hardest time accepting? Is this feature of yourself something you can change, or is it something that is truly beyond your control? Has this difficulty with self-acceptance translated into problems with intimacy? Spend five to ten minutes beaming love toward yourself, especially that part of yourself that you have the hardest time accepting.

59

Everyone has a road not taken in life, that nagging sense that life could have been better or different *if only I'd...* These things tend to come up at the major junctures in life: at middle age, when a marriage or major relationship goes south, when some major health issue appears. The door never slams shut on old dreams; they just slowly fade away. It doesn't hurt to revisit old interests and give them a try. One can always pick up golf without necessarily making it into the PGA tour or practice guitar without aiming to perform in front of a sold-out crowd.

In the realm of relationships, just because you didn't spend the rest of your life with someone doesn't mean that you didn't have something special at one point in time. It is okay to sometimes be curious about what an old flame is doing these days; this curiosity doesn't mean that you are going to burn your life to the ground to go back to that person. It is understandable to miss the good things from the past, even while acknowledging that the past is not going to come roaring back. It's okay to reminisce once in a while, so long as a retreat into the past doesn't become a deep regret that interferes with the present.

We don't actually have to make a hard break with the past or forget about the past in order to move forward in life. Those past experiences made us the people that we are today. As long as we don't inordinately focus on old experiences, we can continue to learn and grow as people. Occasionally some disappointing or tragic experience will linger for years or even decades, to the point where it is difficult to let go. In these sorts of situations, it is good to seek professional help so that events long gone are no longer a hindrance.

You are never really done with the feeling that things could have been different, but the fact is that you freely chose the life that you have now. Rather than looking upon that as a lack or limitation, you can focus on the freedoms and joys that you have available to you as a direct result of the choices that you made. Just as you may regret certain decisions, you also made some good choices and opened lots of possibilities through dedicated effort over the years. It does no good to linger on what you cannot change.

ACTION STEP

Make a list of five things that you appreciate about the life that you have now. Then make a list of five choices that led you to the place in life where you find yourself. What choices could you make now that would land you in a better place in five or ten years?

60

In East Asian culture, dragons are symbols of power and good luck. The dragon's undulating body follows a sine curve of ups and downs, peaks and valleys; this reminds us that the path to success will be filled with triumphs as well as disappointments. The dragon's many legs and wings remind us that we have to work on many fronts to find the fulfillment that we seek. It will not do to focus on work alone or family alone or health alone. We have to honor many different duties all at once.

I recently had the opportunity to visit the Belz Museum of Asian and Judaic Art in Memphis, Tennessee, where I saw more jade dragons than I ever thought possible. Several jade mountain sculptures, each as tall as me, were decorated with intricate pine trees and flowing streams, little hillsides filled with spirits, gods, and sages holding court. Each sculpture must have taken thousands of hours of work and was worth an ungodly amount of money. I was reminded of the Buddha lands of the Pure Land school and of certain stories from India where heroes accidentally stumble upon the kingdom of Kubera, the god of wealth.

Most of us will never get to live in an imperial court, but we can encounter treasures of our own. These treasures can be cultural in nature: finding a good concert venue, library, or museum. Or they can pertain to relationships: having a good group of friends, a strong family life, or great coworkers. And then there are the actual material treasures: maybe we can't all be Bill Gates, but we can dabble in stocks or collect gemstones or do whatever makes us feel abundant. Abundance is local to each place and particular to each circumstance: there is no place and no situation so barren that some form of abundance cannot be found.

I have spent a lot of time in Appalachia, and, even though the region has more than its share of poverty, it has also produced unique cultural forms, like bluegrass music. One can say the same thing of the origins of Mississippi's Delta blues, which made its way to Chicago and then became rock and roll. Hardship and art go hand and hand, so none of us really have an excuse. We just have to find our own forms of wealth, our own jade mountains.

ACTION STEP

What activities or places make you feel abundant? What aspects of your life make you feel lucky to live where you live at this point in your life? Spend a few minutes feeling thankful for the good things in your life, for the positive aspects of your own hometown.

61

The one thing that most of us do wrong is to proceed in fits and starts, to work in bursts of energy followed by days or weeks of nothing. This kind of vacillation, more than anything else, will bring any project grinding to a halt, whether it is a report for work, a plan of exercise, a writing project, or pretty much any significant undertaking. It is very difficult to keep up a large daily quota when some days have big zeros attached to them. It is just the mathematics of averages that a little bit every day will be better in the long run than on-again, off-again efforts.

I teach college students, but I still have a very hard time hammering this point home. So many of my students seem to think that if they just cram for the midterm and the final, they can still do well in the class. This almost never proves to be the case. Without fail, the students who come to class every session are the very same students who make good grades and, more importantly, actually understand the material. Consistency is worth more than intensity, and it is probably also worth more than innate ability. Every time we have something big to tackle, we need to plug away at it every day.

Gradually, these little efforts begin to amount to something. It becomes a little less difficult to go for a run or a little less of a challenge to sit down at the computer to write. Each day's effort builds on the day before in a snowball effect. The voices of doubt and criticism grow less intimidating, and suddenly what seemed impossible lies within reach. The real slayer of inertia is not passion but discipline. And it doesn't have to be freakish discipline or robotic discipline. It also doesn't have to be perfect. One or two missed days doesn't ruin the effect, but missing days habitually does.

There are really only two things to be done in life. The first and the most difficult is to discover what is the most important thing to you, what gets you going. This is difficult because of all the noise, the conflicting cultural messages that get in the way. The second thing to be done is to get on a regimen of daily effort. After that, maybe success comes and maybe it doesn't. If success comes—and success can be defined in dozens of different ways—great. If it doesn't come, that's fine too; there is no shame in trying and failing. The real loss lies in not trying at all.

ACTION STEP

At what time in your life were you the most in the groove with regard to daily effort? How did it feel to keep coming back to the same project, day after day? How can you recapture that feeling in your life right now? What projects could benefit from some steady effort?

62

Another big hindrance in life is caused by the absence of trust. When problems occur, we sometimes form in our mind the mistaken belief that things will continue to go wrong. For example, if we have problems in one romantic relationship, we have a tendency to shrink back and believe that the same problem will occur in the next relationship. Or in the realm of work, if one boss or supervisor was stingy and abusive, we might fear the same circumstances on the next job. If trust is not restored, the same dynamic will keep playing out, and our capacities will shrink until we are much diminished as people.

We are now in the midst of a society-wide loss of trust. Institutions like big banks have been caught defrauding their customers. Car companies cheat on emissions standards. Government officials seem craven and immoral. The entertainment and news industries have been plagued by sexual harassment scandals. It might be easy at this point to just give up on society. But the fact remains that we are social animals, and we have to learn to live with one another and find the good parts of imperfect institutions.

It can feel risky to place our trust in other people, whether we are talking about romantic partners, business partners, or the leaders of big institutions like government or corporations. And indeed it can be risky to trust in people and institutions, but going it alone is far more risky. It is still better to put money in the bank than to shove it under the mattress, still more emotionally satisfying to have good relationships than to be a hermit in the woods. In short, we have to keep putting trust out there into the world; without trust, we become dysfunctional as people and as a civilization.

The opposite of a paranoid mind is a mind that believes the world is trustworthy. Having this basic trust in the goodness of the world catapults life to a higher level. If you believe that you can trust in the world, that you will be supported, then you are free to put your creative abilities to use. You know that you will find help when you go out on a limb and try something new. Believing that people are basically good allows you to step outside of self-protective behaviors and express your true self. You become more vulnerable, yes, but also more prosperous, as you let your deepest visions take shape in reality.

ACTION STEP

Congratulations! You have now made it through more than two-thirds of this challenge. Are you still holding back in some way? Do you believe that you can trust in this process, that your efforts will be rewarded? Take an inventory of your practice so far, and see if there are some places where you can put forth a little more effort toward improving your own life. Know that every bit of diligence you put into this challenge will be rewarded many times over.

63

Remember that the problems that worry you today will seem insignificant five or ten years from now. The possessions that you want today will one day be sold at a yard sale or an estate sale. Your work, too, no matter how well you perform it, will be a product of its time and place. Everything changes, and nothing is exempt from the entropy of the universe. But here is the critical juncture: we can take that impermanence, as it is called in Buddhist thought, and think of it as something depressing, or we can make something beautiful of it.

I know that I will have a finite number of days on this earth, and I am not aware of the exact number. Could be that I will live until I am eighty or a hundred, and it could be that I will die next week. I could get depressed about this and lament the human condition. But there is also an opposite response: I could take it all as a celebration, as a burst of color that blooms like a firework and then fades into ashes.

The finitude of existence actually makes it possible to enjoy life. Eating a cone of ice cream would not be enjoyable if the cone were actually bottomless. My favorite flavor is butter pecan, but if I had to eat butter pecan ice cream all day every day, it would get old pretty quickly. Although we have a limit placed on the amount of enjoyment we can have at a given time, that limit is actually desirable, because it allows us to come down before going back up again.

Hunger makes eating more enjoyable. Work makes rest feel deserved. Bitter experiences make us appreciate the good times. And so on. We want the good without the bad, but if we look more closely, we see why the bad is necessary. And since good and bad revolve around one another, they are not actually separate or opposite. When you have found your balance in life, you no longer have to chase after what you consider good and avoid what you consider bad. It is one thing to realize this in theory and quite another thing to live this, however.

ACTION STEP

Name one challenging condition in your life. Then describe three positive outcomes that have resulted from this circumstance. (Here are some examples: car trouble led to riding a bike to work. Losing a job left more time with children. Bad financial decisions resulted in gaining money management skills.)

64

We tend to fear things that we want to escape, but we don't realize that fear actually binds the thing or circumstance feared closer to us. The things that we fear follow us. People who are not afraid of spiders don't go around thinking about spiders or looking for spiders. Fear of spiders is paradoxically a specific type of spider obsession. We conjure up the fear to get away from something, and we keep on doing it, over and over again, even though this routine doesn't save us. Each instance of fear only confirms the fear habit, making it stronger over time.

We can't get rid of fear by just fleeing from the big scary thing. Because fear is manifested in the psyche, it doesn't go away by simply changing the external circumstances. Someone who is afraid of clowns could avoid going to the circus, but that person still may dream of clowns at night. We have to get around fear by taming or mastering it, to put ourselves back in the driver's seat. We have to make ourselves big and the thing that we fear very small. This means neither avoiding what we fear nor giving undue attention to it.

A kid might fear crashing on her bike, and she overcomes that fear only by learning how to ride the bike. We can get over our own fears in the same way: by learning how to effectively deal with the troubling circumstances. This can happen only very gradually, as fears that have become deep-seated have almost become hardwired through repetition. It will take a lot of positive reinforcement to get rid of the years of negative reinforcement.

We can overcome our fears by taking baby steps, like learning to swim in the shallow end of the pool and then graduating to the deep end over time. As adults, our fears get more abstract: we may fear going bankrupt or fear the loss of family members or fear some catastrophic health problem. Even though these are big abstractions, we can still prepare for them. We can take rational and reasonable steps like taking insurance policies and planning for retirement. These are not phobic responses; they are just preparations for the scenarios that could arise.

ACTION STEP

Do you have fears that have followed you for years? Instead of continuing to practice avoidance, take some concrete steps to face your fear. Start with "shallow end" strategies. If you are afraid of public speaking, you could give a speech in front of a mirror, and then present it to one of your best friends, and then two friends, and so on. See if this step-by-step approach applies to your particular fear.

65

When you really need to get something done, there is no substitute for setting aside all distraction. Put your cell phone in another room, disconnect from the Internet, and disable notifications on your computer. Use an app like Pomodoro to time your work in twenty-five-minute intervals with five-minute breaks in between. Do not leave the work area to check the mail or get a cup of coffee. Allow yourself a fifteen-minute break only after you have completed four twenty-five-minute sessions.

Another tip that bears repeating: email is one of the biggest time sucks at most workplaces. Simply deleting extraneous emails can take hours. To save time, let your email auto-archive the old items. Use folders for the essential stuff, and leave everything else there in the main feed. If you are having trouble finding something, use the search function. Do a big purge two times per year using the mass delete functions of your email system. You can purge every email before a certain date, block certain spam senders, and unsubscribe from mailing lists.

Next, social media is a valuable way to connect with people, but it shouldn't be an A-level priority all the time unless you are working on a campaign for your job. Set aside a block or two during the day for checking your favorite feeds. Make this a sort of treat for after you have gotten some important things done. The same goes for checking news sites and other favorite locations on the web. Make this type of Internet browsing a resting activity reserved for genuine downtime.

Now I will throw a counterintuitive suggestion into the mix. Read books every day, even if you aren't exactly sure how they fit into your work. Let your curiosity guide you within your chosen field and also make sure to read outside your field. It doesn't matter that much whether you are reading fiction or nonfiction, serious or humorous. This will be enriching activity that you will not regret; worry about the practical applications later.

ACTION STEP

Try using the Pomodoro method of work today. Download a project management app like KanbanFlow (which includes the Pomodoro timer) or just use the timer on your phone. Work for twenty-five minutes, then take a five-minute break. After four rounds of this, you may then take a fifteen-minute break. See how much you are able to accomplish using this technique.

66

Gratitude doesn't always come easily, especially when we experience tough times and low emotional states. And yet gratitude also serves as a remedy for those very same sad feelings and difficult experiences. In order to improve your sense of gratitude, you have to work at it, just like learning any other skill. You have to build the gratitude muscles by practicing a little bit every day, and then you find yourself also feeling more positive about life.

Gratitude does not have to be profound, and it does not have to be directed toward God or something external. Gratitude practice is the cultivation of an inward attitude of appreciation for the good things in life. Gratitude can be directed toward the small things: the cup of herbal tea on my desk, the fact that my computer has not crashed recently, the fact that I got the oil changed in my car. I simply call to mind aspects of life that I am enjoying right now. As I think of one thing to appreciate, it naturally leads to others.

It is also okay to repeat some of the same things, day after day. I am grateful for my family every day. I am grateful for my home every day. I am grateful for food and drink every day. These daily recollections serve as a reminder that we have a large amount of stability in our lives that is not available to everyone. Then we begin to sense compassion for those who may be experiencing much more difficult circumstances than we do.

Gratitude leads to a change in worldview, a movement from an attitude of entitlement to an attitude of joyful acceptance. Gratitude also shifts interactions with others, as we genuinely appreciate what they bring to our lives. We find ourselves practicing more kindness and showing affection more easily. Our emotional states soften, and we become less defensive. Gratitude is an inner revolution, an intentional shift toward harmony with the world.

ACTION STEP

Have you been doing the gratitude exercise described in Part 1 every day? If you have not, go ahead and enter a space of calm contemplation, and mentally list two "big" things and two "small" things for which you feel grateful today. As you do this exercise, see if you notice any emotional shifts. See also how your attitude toward others might be changing.

67

If our core thoughts are bold and dynamic, our lives will fall in line behind them. But if our core thoughts are shriveled whimpers, our lives will similarly atrophy. We have to remain vigilant against these forms of bad thinking, because bad thoughts lead to bad actions, which lead to bad outcomes.

To do well in life, we have to summon courage and enthusiasm, not just once but again and again and in all times and places. If we allow ourselves to go back into old, lackadaisical habits, the progress made thus far disappears as well. We fight first against our own inertia and then against entropy. We tend the lush garden of thought by practicing care for our minds, by working ever so diligently for mental peace and abundance. To paraphrase the book of James (3:4), a small rudder steers a big ship; just so, the thoughts of our minds make our lives fall into good or bad patterns.

If we cannot still our minds, we will not be able to still a tumultuous life. If we cannot find fulfillment within, we will not be able to find fulfillment without. The small space between the ears governs the large, outside space. Fix one and fix the other. Will change in one and master the other. A distracted person tumbles through life, from disaster to disaster; an alert person grows stronger even in the midst of challenging circumstances.

We have to utterly defeat anxiety and passivity. We have to become the heroes we were born to be. We have to be completely finished with small dramas and small thoughts so that we might become truly noble people. We must believe that we are more than capable of tackling everything that life throws at us. We become larger than any difficulty, stronger than any challenge, brighter than any dark place.

ACTION STEP

What bad mental habits hold you back from getting what you want in life? Take five minutes and cultivate the exact opposite feeling or sentiment, imagining what it would be like to have the opposite frame of mind. If you have a tendency to be suspicious of people, spend five minutes cultivating acceptance and trust. If you have a tendency toward sadness, spend five minutes thinking only of joy. See how you feel after five minutes of intense effort.

68

The boundless life is all about overcoming self-imposed limitations. We have to acknowledge that much of what we consider to be natural hindrances or shortcomings are actually imposed by our own minds. If I tell myself that I'm not good at math, that will become true for me. I can even refer to my family tree, saying *my dad was not good at math, and his dad was not good at math*, and so forth. But this is just a way of justifying a falsehood that actually lies completely within my control.

We have many beliefs that we think arise from our fundamental natures, when they are really creations of our own thoughts and habits. If I tell myself that I am not good with people, that will lead to social isolation, which will lead to a lack of practice with social interaction, which will lead to a deterioration in my social skills. Through this self-defeating cycle, I am creating the very thing that I told myself was naturally part of my makeup. We tend to blame nature when it is our own actions that are at fault.

The line between nature and nurture is quite fuzzy, and there are complex interactions between biology and environment. Most traits involve family history, environmental factors, and group socialization. But even the supposedly inalterable, natural factors are perceived through the prism of thoughts and behaviors. I can alter nature itself by how I perceive it. Nothing is finally fixed, because my mind is itself part of nature and has causal efficacy.

The Price Is Right game show has a Plinko game in which a token falls down through rows of pegs and into one of the slots at the bottom of the board. One slot might win a contestant a new dinette set or a new Ford Mustang, while another one would lead to no more than a few cans of tuna or a new vacuum cleaner. We make the mistake of thinking that our lives are like that. We think that once we let go of the token (i.e., once we make certain major life choices), the token will land where it will. In other words, we think we have a limited amount of control, and the rest is left to nature. In reality, we can keep intervening in the game at all stages. We can nudge the token this way and that the whole time. Artifice and nature are not opposites; we control them both.

ACTION STEP

Do you have some limitations that you believe are natural that really may be a product of your own thoughts and actions? What stories do you tell yourself about your own abilities? Take at least one thing that you believe you cannot do and convince yourself that the opposite is true.

69

At the end of the day, we can't control other people's behavior or intuit their intentions. As a way to assuage the uncertainties related to this fact, we may try to purchase love and affection through care-taking behavior and people-pleasing behavior. These attempts often backfire as we fail to dedicate ourselves to the things that we truly value. The people who are recipients of our caretaking and placating may even come to resent the attention that we lavish on them. The situation that results leaves no one very happy.

We are far better off simply making decisions for ourselves and finding that course of action where we think personal happiness lies. This means occasionally being labeled as selfish or insensitive, but it stands a much greater chance of taking us to the place where we wish to be in life. We also give our loved ones a little more space for their own projects and plans, so that they can have some independence. Perfect love does not mean that one person sacrifices all for another; it means that both people feel fulfilled and respected.

There is nothing wrong with demonstrating our love for the people in our lives, so long as we do not give to the point of feeling burdened and resentful. At that point, we begin to cut into our own sense of purpose and are practicing a bad sort of self-sacrifice. And our loved ones can detect the difference between something freely given and something given out of a feeling of duty or obligation. Life is more enjoyable for everyone when no one acts from a spirit of martyrdom and self-effacement.

Even though we strive for self-expression and fulfillment, we should always practice skill and kindness in the way that we treat others. We can say no to the people in our lives without doing so in a mean or condescending way. We can express our own preferences without belittling the preferences of others. When we do things honestly but kindly, things flow along much more smoothly. This will not guarantee a life without conflict, but it ensures that any disputes that arise will be handled with care.

ACTION STEP

Take some time today to do what you want to do, rather than just taking care of everyone else. Spend an hour in a pursuit that is meaningful to you and does not involve fulfilling work or household duties.

70

Transitioning to a new mode of being requires the pain of getting used to unfamiliar places, things, and circumstances. We often shrink back from change specifically because we do not want the pain that goes along with it. But we will have pain whether we move forward or stay in one place. The key is to learn to appreciate what the pain is telling you.

Trying to get rid of pain is far worse than learning to live with it. When we try to avoid pain, we suddenly have to adopt a host of bad coping strategies, turning to self-medication rather than simply sitting with the hurt and the loss. Pain can be a good companion if we let it be: it shows us where we have been hurt, it tells us where to concentrate our efforts, and it ultimately directs us toward healing. Pain is a sign of life, both the life that we are now living and the life waiting to be born.

By living with pain, I do not mean the sort of superman muscling through pain that is pretty common in sports. I mean learning to accept that pain is a part of life, and that we don't necessarily have to do anything about it. Sometimes the treatment for pain is worse than the pain itself. If we just sit with pain and be patient with it, we can receive its message. It may be that we can find some corrective measure for a pain-wracked mind and body, one that doesn't require extreme measures.

We can find the message that the pain conveys by listening deeply, whether the discomfort is physical or mental in nature. If I am feeling sad, what sort of sadness is it? Is it a mournful longing, an acute disappointment, or a lasting melancholy? If I have a bodily pain, is it dull and aching or sharp and throbbing? Is it localized to one region or more general? When we unravel the message of pain, we have a better idea of how to move forward. We will know whether to rest or to keep going, whether to seek treatment or to just give it time.

ACTION STEP

Take a look at the pain that you experience in your own life, whether that pain is physical or mental in nature (or it may be a combination of the two). Has this pain or the fear of pain held you back from realizing what you want in life? Go into a mode of close observation and see what you can learn by simply sitting with whatever feelings you have.

71

We all have a bias toward the familiar, with a tendency to believe that things will be in the future the way they have been in the past. This is known in philosophy as the principle of conservative induction: we simply look at the data from our past experience and extrapolate forward to project future outcomes. But reality does not always conform to past experience; the unexpected happens on a regular basis. We will never be able to understand events before they happen, using either complicated statistical methods or a deck of tarot cards.

This unpredictability of the future has huge implications for living a boundless life. In the past, we have had the tendency to shrink from the unpredictable future, to hunker down in fear of the storms to come. But this unpredictability also means that incomparably good things await on the horizon, that we may not yet have experienced the best that life has to offer. The satisfying, blissful experiences that have touched us in life thus far represent only a small taste of what the universe has to offer.

We have all tasted something of the wonder and joy of living, if only for a second or two. These glimpses tell us that the life that we desire is completely possible. The world does not conspire against our plans or deliberately withhold rewards from us. The distribution of the satisfactions of life may be uneven, but we are guaranteed to reach at least some satisfaction if we persevere long enough. We just have to be dogged and determined enough to keep pursuing our plans even when it seems nothing will come of them.

Think about making a batch of chocolate chip cookies. There will always be one cookie that has only one or two chocolate chips, and another cookie that is loaded with chips. It might be nice if all of the cookies had the exact same number of chips, but the one with only one or two chips is still pretty good. As we go through life, some periods will be loaded with both intrinsic and extrinsic rewards, and other periods will feel dull and dry. But if we just keep going, we find the sweetness that we desire.

ACTION STEP

Are you projecting your future based on disappointing experiences from the past? Name one area where you have experienced a lot of frustrations. Now imagine what life would be like if the past conditions changed entirely. Spend a few minutes picturing life entirely without the blockages that hindered you in the past.

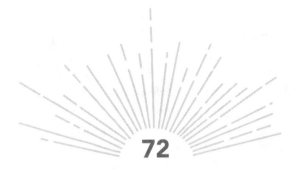

72

One of the everyday miracles that we easily overlook is the human propensity to experience setbacks, even disastrous ones, and still recover and try again. As we make our way through the world encountering total strangers—on the subway, getting coffee, in the checkout line—we come so close to hidden triumphs and tragedies. We have to remember that we never fully know the struggles behind the expressions on the faces of the people we meet.

Humankind is capable of great things in terms of technological feats, like landing humans on the moon or sending rovers to Mars, but this everyday resilience gives our species its true strength. In the end, our ability to form bonds with one another, to find novel solutions to complex problems, and to bear any adversity will propel us toward a more harmonious world. We are part and parcel of life on earth, and life is very tenacious. It doesn't let go easily.

We all live through major life tragedies and normal wear-and-tear incidents, like fender benders and spilled coffee. Each time we gather our resources, summon our courage, and go back out there. This capacity to recover from adverse conditions defines us as living beings, and it will see us through any difficulty. This tendency toward equilibrium resides in us quite naturally; we just need to allow life to express itself within us.

The will to live does not have to be a drive to dominate other people. Life only requires a niche of its own. When you deliberately will yourself to keep going after a big or small rough patch, you tap into the drive toward life that exists in the cosmos as a whole. Your striving is completely natural, and it manifests itself in new forms of thinking and doing. Each time you put yourself out there, a new set of possibilities unfolds.

ACTION STEP

Have you had a minor or major mishap recently—in your health, career, or relationships? It is normal to feel a little shell-shocked when things go wrong, but eventually the time comes when you need to let go of the past and try again. Find one way today that you can recover lost momentum in a troubled area of your life.

73

Our culture has gone astray by placing too much emphasis on monetary value. The intrinsic worth of a forest can't be measured in the quantity of lumber it contains. Anyone who walks in the woods with an open heart knows this intuitively. In the same way, we cannot assign value to people based on their salaries or net worth. Some highly destructive people in this world are well compensated, and some who contribute immeasurably to future generations struggle just to pay the bills.

We have to let go of market value as a way of measuring things. When we strip away this false form of valuation, all people appear before us on the same plane. No one is worth more than anyone else because of the clothes they wear or the car they drive or the size of their 401(k). In this vision of things, we can see people for the qualities that they put forward, whether they are kind or generous or capable. We grow more appreciative of the everyday people who make the world go around.

The tech CEOs, the celebrity class, and the finance pundits get a lot of media attention, but much of this adulation is undeserved. A large portion of success is due to being in the right place at the right time. This is not to say that these people are not talented, only that they do not deserve to be accorded superhuman status or given undue power and influence. Every human being has innate talent and intelligence; everyone deserves a chance to succeed in life. The more we believe in basic equality, the more our societies advance toward fairness.

As we detach from addiction to celebrity, we pay more attention to our own abilities. We realize that we can create our own entertainment and cultivate our own talents. We take more ownership of our own destinies and make brighter futures for ourselves. We use the power that we have to make our lives fuller and brighten the days of those around us. We enjoy the company of others and work to create a better world.

ACTION STEP

As you go through your day today, make sure to smile and say thank you to everyone you meet. Do one kind thing for a stranger before the end of the day.

74

As we look at ourselves in the mirror, it can be all too easy to concentrate on the parts of ourselves that we do not like, to look at the flab or the wrinkles or the scars. We spend so much time policing the disliked aspects of our appearance that we do not notice the good qualities that we have going for us. It can be hard to correct this distorted view after years of self-criticism, especially for those of us who have struggled with body dysphoria or eating disorders. To get over this habitual criticism of the body, we have to practice a lot of self-love and even exaggerate the love that we show for our own bodies.

One of the first things that we do each morning is look in the mirror, and, unfortunately, we often start with something pretty negative, thinking *I look like hell* or *Look at those bags under my eyes.*

This negative self-talk starts the trajectory for the day on the wrong footing and leads to a negative frame of mind with regard to our embodiment. This then spills over into other areas, leading to a lack of self-confidence and an inability to take the initiative in decision-making. It is well worth the effort to stop negative thoughts about the body and change this dynamic.

We should all begin to keep a list of things we like about our physical appearance. Everyone has good qualities that are quite natural and long-lasting. Maybe you have nice skin or good hair. Maybe you like your curves or your butt. Maybe you like your muscles and your physical strength. Maybe you have good balance or good stamina. Maybe you have long eyelashes or beautiful eyes. Taking the time to notice and appreciate these things will go a long way toward body acceptance.

This is not to say that you shouldn't take steps to change the things about your physical appearance that you do not like. There is nothing wrong with changing fashions and hairstyles or makeup and physical fitness. We should just use these tools as steps toward body acceptance rather than using them as a form of punishment. If some beauty secret makes you feel better about yourself, by all means use it! But we still need to do the inner work of practicing self-love, without which all of the aesthetic changes won't make any difference.

ACTION STEP

When you have a chance, stand before a full-length mirror and look your body up and down. Find five positive things to say about yourself while directing feelings of love and acceptance toward your body. If you catch yourself directing an insulting comment toward some aspect of your appearance, start over again at one.

75

Things that we leave undone have a way of sticking with us, lurking there in the back corners of the mind. Procrastination acts like a slow energy drain, subtly preventing full engagement with the present. When enough tasks are left undone, we begin to feel frazzled and off-kilter. Eventually we might suffer a loss of reputation as our clients, customers, and coworkers might begin to see us as unreliable. To avoid this situation, we have to periodically do a major push to clean up the to-do list, to make sure that the most important items are completed.

Working twelve-hour days every day does not really accomplish what we want. Anyone working this hard is either being exploited or is doing a lot of busywork or both. We don't want our schedules to be cluttered with a bunch of junk items. If it is something that is work-related but uninteresting and unsatisfying, it should be completed as quickly as possible. If it is work-related but satisfying and interesting, it is okay to linger over that task. We should gauge our time expenditure by the amount of satisfaction that we take in each aspect of the work.

This may sound out of touch or impractical, but most people have at least some wiggle room in the performance of job duties. We also have different strengths and abilities, so two people in the exact same job will respond quite differently to the situations they encounter. Good supervisors will not try to have complete uniformity, as this blunts the creative individuality that makes work fun and interesting. As we reflect on our own working lives, we should try to make sure that we are prioritizing the right tasks, so that we feel both productive and satisfied.

Part of job satisfaction lies in having the right job, but an even greater part lies in how you approach the work. Rather than looking on each task as onerous and burdensome, try to find a small space of creativity and freedom. This will be impossible if you are constantly behind on the job, always playing catch-up. Instead, try to work quickly and efficiently, especially when the task at hand is not in your main area of concern. When you perform the small things with efficiency, this leaves more time for the items that you enjoy the most.

ACTION STEP

Make a list of the parts of your job that you love the most. If you can, rearrange your schedule so that you are spending more time with what you love. If you don't have control over your schedule, consider having a meeting with your supervisor so that you can get time reassigned to the tasks that are most interesting to you.

76

If you suffer from long-standing mental health problems, like anxiety and depression, take the time to get treatment if you have not already done so. Having a therapist or possibly pharmaceutical interventions can make a world of difference in how you feel. There are also lots of skills to be gained in therapy, like learning to better communicate with loved ones and exploring suppressed feelings.

As valuable as psychotherapy or psychiatry can be, we have to recognize that counselors and medical practitioners do not have all the answers. They may help us to discover the action steps that we need to take, but we have to actually tackle the problems on our own. We also have to bring something to the therapeutic relationship, to be willing to ask questions and dig deeply, taking notes when necessary. The whole time, we remain active participants, taking charge of our own care and making decisions for our own well-being.

We also have to keep doing the regular maintenance work on our lives if we are to have the happiness that we seek. Happiness is enabled by eating a good diet, exercising daily, and practicing meditation. We also need to keep a watchful eye over all aspects of life, maintaining our relationships and using time wisely. When we do these regular maintenance activities, the medical or psychological interventions will be much more effective. We need modern medicine, but we also have to do the everyday self-care to make ourselves feel good. When we take the best of holistic health and combine that with scientific understanding, we give ourselves the best chance for happiness and well-being.

ACTION STEP

If you suffer from an ongoing illness, whether mental or physical, have you sought treatment for your problem? If conventional medicine hasn't worked for you, have you tried alternative therapies? Conversely, if you have looked into natural remedies but they don't seem to be working, would you consider going to a doctor?

77

Social connections buoy our progress in life. Just talking with a friend about a problem makes the problem easier to bear. But sometimes we get so caught in our own routines that we lose connections with our friends. For those who struggle with social anxiety, this tendency to disconnect can be even deeper. Sometimes we don't want to step outside the confines of our comfortable spaces to connect with people, even though we actually crave that contact.

It can be easy to get caught in fear of social situations, worrying excessively about saying the wrong thing or wearing the wrong outfit. Most of the time, people barely notice these little gaffes, and, if they do, it usually will be a minor hiccup. The other guests at a party have their own game to think about, and they are also invested in minimizing awkwardness. The feeling of being in the spotlight, the feeling of being watched and scrutinized, is usually just an illusion.

Social anxiety easily carries over into digital spaces; we can get caught up in how many likes we get on a post or checking to see who has the most followers. Sometimes people can be meaner online than they would be in real life, because of the added distance and anonymity. We don't have to remain in spaces that make us feel unwelcome or unsafe. We don't have to be super-users, nor do we have to unplug entirely. We just need to find the right balance in online communication.

Communication also takes place within the home, and this is arguably the most important area. You might occasionally feel afraid to express your true feeling around a partner because of a fear of conflict. This lack of communication doesn't make problems go away; it actually postpones dealing with them or even compounds them. In order to be close with other people, you have to open yourself to them, whether the topic of conversation is lighthearted or serious. The more you are willing to give of yourself, the more you receive in return.

ACTION STEP

Have you lost touch with someone you care about? Take a few minutes today to give them a call or send a text.

78

Spirituality does not have to mean organized religion, although it certainly can. We all need a belief system that helps us to find meaning in our lives and a sense of wonder at the good things in our lives. Some people find that higher purpose by going out into nature, others through study of science, and some through traditional beliefs and practices. We just need a reason to get out of bed in the morning, a way of thinking and living that makes us feel both challenged and supported.

We may find ourselves gradually stepping away from the belief systems that we inherited and exploring different world philosophies. I think this is a perfectly normal part of maturing as a person. We retain the things that we like about our childhood beliefs, and we get rid of the things that we find to be oppressive or restrictive. As we develop as people, we branch into new belief systems and test different ways of viewing the world. Without this sort of curious inquiry, life becomes dull and stagnant.

Dogmatic beliefs stunt natural curiosity and make this open-ended inquiry difficult, and one can have a hidebound atheistic belief just as one can be stridently religious. Good beliefs feel freeing and open-ended: they do not ask us to abandon our ethical or intellectual principles. If a particular belief leads to a sense of being controlled or manipulated, it must fall by the wayside to make room for a more capacious worldview. We can discern manipulative belief systems, because they are coercive and imply a threat either in this lifetime or in some future state.

To have the boundless life that you seek, you have to seriously inquire into how you see the world and make adjustments. If you view life as one of dog-eat-dog struggle, or as a vale of tears, or as a form of punishment, it will be pretty difficult to find a sense of joy and abundance. To have freedom in life, you have to claim it for yourself, to reject beliefs that encourage repression and guilt. At the same time, you have to honor the responsibilities that you have and balance individualism with community.

ACTION STEP

Spend a few minutes journaling about a specific instance where your faith or worldview hindered you in life. If you have time, write about your current beliefs and ask whether or not they support what you want to achieve in life.

79

As we age, we might develop chronic pain and tricky joints, scars and injuries that make it more difficult to be physically active. It can be tempting to just cater to the pain and limit our activities to the point where there is less discomfort. Unfortunately, giving in to the debility over the long term only gives us less range of motion and makes our health deteriorate even further. The only way to recover full use of our bodies is to gradually become more active and put creaky joints back to use.

Sitting at a desk all day is about the worst possible thing for our spines and circulation, with sitting on the couch or in a recliner a close second. Paying attention to posture and ergonomics can go a long way toward reducing pain, but it is also important to take frequent breaks during the day to get up and move around. Even at home, use a stationary bike if you have one on those days you can't exercise outside. Walking the dog or doing yoga are also good ways to get in some low-impact exercise.

A sedentary body leads to low emotional states, proneness to ailments, and less vibrant thought processes. Mental and physical health are completely intertwined; we can't have one without the other.

If you get out of restrictive modes of life, like being sedentary, you free yourself for self-care. You can focus on what really benefits your body and mind. Holistic wellness frees you from compulsions and makes possible a new way of life that brings health to mind and body.

ACTION STEP

Do you have bodily pains that prevent you from pursuing an active life? If you truly have an unaddressed injury, make an appointment today to see a physical therapist or primary care provider. Otherwise, work with your doctor to find forms of exercise that don't overly tax the injury. Swimming, walking, and yoga might be good options.

80

Every organization has a large number of workers who do the minimum amount possible to collect a paycheck. They go home at the end of the day and think nothing of it. Then there are some moderately conscientious workers who do a good job but don't go out of their way to take on additional projects. And then another small segment of workers does most of the work, coming up with new ideas and going above and beyond. This small portion of highly functional people really make things happen, but they are the employees most prone to burnout.

This disparity in the level of commitment in the workforce exists in just about every workplace, whether it's a for-profit or nonprofit organization. Every manager would like to have more highly motivated people on the team, but even a mediocre employee has a role to play, as part of the social glue that holds things together. The main thing is that everyone should feel appreciated for what he or she brings to the table, even if that level of contribution is different for each person. Everyone deserves a workplace in which they feel valued and respected.

If you have invested a lot of time and energy into your professional life, you may feel overlooked and undervalued at times. In the absence of a pay raise or a promotion on the horizon, do what you can to take care of yourself on the job. Avoid accepting responsibilities not listed in your job description, and try not to bring work home. Set boundaries on checking email and taking phone calls outside of working hours. This will feel uncomfortable at first, but your coworkers will soon accept your boundaries and respect them.

Some simple routines will help your workday to feel like less of a grind and make you feel more satisfied on the job. Take a few minutes at the beginning of the day to do some deep breathing and meditation. Repeat this ritual on your lunch break and before returning home. Keeping a daily calendar and prioritizing tasks can help to reduce stress. Use commute time to listen to positive podcasts or relaxing music while avoiding aggressive driving.

ACTION STEP

As you look at your working life, are you overworking, underworking, or in just the right place? What imbalances do you need to correct? Make a list of three things that you need to do differently.

81

Psychologist Daniel Goleman writes that "in the dance of feeling and thought the emotional faculty guides our moment-to-moment decisions, working hand-in-hand with the rational mind, enabling—or disabling—thought itself. Likewise, the thinking brain plays an executive role in our emotions—except in those moments when...the emotional brain runs rampant." Rationality runs parallel with the emotional life, each strand—the mental and the feeling dimensions—influencing but never fully eclipsing the other.

Western culture has a strong tendency to privilege rationality over the emotions. This tendency also has a sexist bent, as emotions are associated with femininity, and rationality with masculinity. Having a healthy life requires cooperation between the intellect and feelings, not a dictatorship of the rational over the emotional. If we continually try to suppress the emotions, we end up unable to feel the whole range of highs and lows and become numb to life. We need to make friends with the emotions and allow them a place.

In mindfulness meditation, we pay close attention to the feelings that arise, making sure to observe them closely in their particularity. Then we can discern different types or flavors of sadness, joy, anger, and so forth. Only after completely feeling the emotional states do we begin to incorporate them into an understanding of why that emotional state arose in the first place. We come to recognize our emotional triggers through a reflective stance toward our own biographies, not so that we can make the emotions go away, but so that we can come to a constructive relationship with them.

We thus try to avoid two errors, on the one side being blindly carried by the emotions without understanding them, and, on the other side, denying and suppressing the emotions to the point where we dull our sensitivities. In the middle space, we acknowledge and respect the emotions for their valuable contributions, and we integrate the intellectual and the feeling aspects of life into one whole. As we pay more attention to our emotional lives, we understand ourselves better and navigate through the world more easily.

ACTION STEP

Take a look at your own emotional state right now by closing your eyes for a few minutes of meditation. Whether you are experiencing something positive or negative, pay close attention to your feelings. After a few minutes of silent reflection, ask yourself what caused your feelings to arise, either by thinking to yourself or writing in your journal.

82

We can challenge ourselves in our social lives just as we can challenge ourselves in athletics or work. Some people are naturally social beings and easily make dates with friends, throw parties, and go to events and functions. The rest of us bumble along in an awkward way, not knowing how to connect or when to accept an invitation. The fact remains that our social lives are crucial to how we feel as people and have a big impact on the opportunities available to us. We can't afford to opt out of this part of life if we want to have a boundless life.

Challenging ourselves socially will mean different things to different people. For someone with major phobias, simply going out of the house and sitting in a public place will be a major breakthrough. For a social butterfly, expanding the guest list at a party will be a challenge. Most of us, as busy as we are, simply need to reclaim a bit of space for a social life by going out on the town occasionally or inviting friends over for dinner. Allowing space for a social life in our busy world is itself something of a challenge.

When we make room for social connections, we make our lives richer and fuller, expanding and strengthening the web of connections that support our lives. We don't have to wait for a special occasion or a crisis situation to reach out to friends and family. Any average Tuesday will do. We have myriad ways of keeping in touch, from texts to emails to phone calls to (gasp!) postal mail. We can just say hello, invite someone to lunch, or plan an outing. It is much easier to stay in the habit of doing this sort of thing than it is to reconnect after long periods of isolation.

It can be easy to lose touch with friends and family, for months or even years. We begin to rebuild the web of connections one step at a time—a text here, an email there. Taking one small step every day or even every week will be enough to ensure progress. We can gradually accelerate those connections over time, so the process doesn't seem overwhelming. These check-ins can be planned on a calendar, like any other task. That may seem to take the fun out of it, but for most busy people, if it doesn't go on the calendar, it doesn't get done. Making relationships more of a priority can put us back on the path to an abundant life.

ACTION STEP

Get out your calendar and make a plan to reconnect socially. You can make entries like *call Joan*, *send Bob birthday present*, etc. Plan at least one item per week for four weeks.

83

By now, I hope you are getting the idea that the boundless life cannot be found by concentrating on one area alone. We seek to be fully functional, adult human beings in all areas of life at once. We look for vibrant health, sound finances, strong relationships, satisfying work, and deep meaning. Naysayers will retort that it is impossible to have it all, but we reject all forms of cynicism and despair. The life that we seek is within our grasp; we just have to work in a coordinated and disciplined way, challenging ourselves and meeting those challenges.

We let go of habits in our lives that do not help us to live optimally. Think about the sandbags on a hot air balloon; the balloon rises only as the sandbags are released. The sandbags represent the bad habits that we would like to release: negative thinking, poor diet, lack of exercise, and social isolation. The lift on the balloon is produced by burning fuel; we have to exert ourselves in order to reach the heights. We burn fuel by doing physical exercise, trying new things, pursuing creative projects, and reaching out to friends. The burn rate increases as we continually put ourselves out there.

We face hazards along the way. As we get more physical exercise, there is the possibility of injury. In social connections, there is the possibility of rejection. In work, there is the possibility of burnout. Anything that we pursue in life comes with some risk associated; this is just part of the structure of the universe. The worst thing we could possibly do is continually avoid situations of risk out of a fear of failure. The best attitude to cultivate is one of accepting reasonable amounts of risk, knowing that occasionally things will fall flat.

We learn from our failures as much as our successes. There is nothing at all wrong with failure as long as we do not allow ourselves to become permanently discouraged. In athletics, we have to accept that we will not get a personal best every time. In relationships, we will sometimes have bad dates. At work, we will have many days that are boring and routine. The bad days help us to appreciate the good days even more, and they help us to increase our drive and fortitude. The boundless life is made of both triumphs and setbacks.

ACTION STEP

Out of all the areas of responsibility in your life, which one needs the most attention? Is it your finances? Your relationships? Your career? Your social life? Pick one action item that pertains to that neglected area and take that positive step today.

84

Those of us who have grown up with strong religious backgrounds can have a hard time with self-acceptance, because, no matter what we do, it doesn't feel good enough. Because we spent a good chunk of our lives under the eye of an extremely demanding deity, we then become very demanding of ourselves, even when we move along to kinder visions of the divine. Those old habits remain with us throughout life, producing a shadow side of guilt and shame.

To move out from under the shadow of repressive religious beliefs, we have to fight the guiding assumptions upon which those beliefs rest. We have to question the idea that there is something fundamentally sinful in our natures. We have to question the system of eternal rewards and punishments. We have to take a hard look at our God concepts, to make sure they align with what we value in life. Keep in mind we don't have to wholesale reject our childhood beliefs; we just have to place them in suspension and give them a good, critical examination.

Over time, we can de-program ourselves from oppressive religious beliefs. Just like programming a computer, we can debug our operating systems or install new software. As we become more adept, we can keep those features that we like and delete the ones that we don't. The purists and fundamentalists will not approve of this sort of selective approach, but we are the guardians of our own souls. The choices about what we believe are ours to make.

Once you have let go of the all-or-nothing approach, you can experiment with different beliefs, trying them on like new sets of clothing. You can see what fits and what doesn't fit. You may be accused of being shallow or capricious in your beliefs, but these accusations are just more control strategies in disguise. You sift and sort your belief systems to find out which are most affirming and supportive, so that your heart and mind agree, pointing you to an ever-expanding sense of possibility and gratitude.

ACTION STEP

Do you have an overbearing belief system in your past? Think of a time when you felt shamed or controlled on the basis of religious or political doctrine. See if you can root out the source of the shame and find a better place in life.

85

We begin with the bodies we were given at birth, but we can change the expression of that particular embodiment. We have fashion and makeup at our disposal. We can sculpt our bodies through exercise. We can enhance ourselves through bodybuilding or shaping undergarments. New avenues open every day for men, women, and transgender people to find the embodiment that they desire. We need not be bound by what we were given at birth; we can be anyone we want to be. We start with the bodies that we are given, but that is just the starting point, the blank canvas for the people we become.

We have two avenues at our disposal: the first route is body acceptance, practicing loving kindness toward our physical frame. The second route is body modification, changing what we do not like about the body. These two routes should not be viewed as contradictory; we can love the body and modify it at the same time. Indeed, body modification can lead to body acceptance. Self-harming behaviors can be transmuted into body modification and body acceptance. Gradually we learn to love who we are on all levels: physical, mental, and spiritual.

Of course, you can find extreme cases where someone has perhaps gone too far with body modification, but isn't that the case with anything? The vast majority of people are able to pick and choose exactly what they want and go no further than that.

Body modification can result in drastic improvements in self-esteem, which has cascading effects in all areas of life. We should love our bodies, yes, while acknowledging that loving our bodies sometimes means making alterations here and there.

ACTION STEP

Have you ever wanted to pay closer attention to fashion or get a piercing or play with makeup? Is there a problem area of your body that has a relatively easy fix? Take the time today to read a few articles about some change that you would like to make, or go ahead and make an appointment today.

86

If you haven't found your lifelong career yet, that's perfectly fine. Start with what you always dreamed you would be as a kid. If you do have a career already and are feeling stuck where you are, think about the goals that you had when you took your first job. Most likely, you have some unfinished items that still need your attention. We are put in the places where we are, because we still have important work to do.

We live our lives, but our lives also live us. Challenges are put into our paths so that we can puzzle our way through them. Sometimes this means taking action in the external world, and sometimes it means making some changes within. Sometimes we may be through with a particular place or experience, but someone else may really need our contributions. When we live as our freaky, wonderful selves, we both carry out our own missions in life and give to the world what it needs the most.

What we most need to avoid is shrinking into a more acceptable, more tame version of ourselves. We have to stop giving people what we think they want and start living as the people we know ourselves to be. *Authenticity* is a tricky word, and maybe we don't really know what it means, but we should always be in the process of trying to discern what we were meant to do on this earth. We can't let people and circumstances dictate to us what we were meant to be; we have to be guided by dreams and visions, hunches and intuitions.

This may sound like fragile, mystical stuff, but these slender threads of the spiritual life guide us into the deep and satisfying places. When we have an intuition about the best way to live our lives, whether on the job or in personal matters, we have to go with that suggestion, no matter how odd it might seem. We need practicality and spirituality; both types of reflection will help you live a well-ordered and satisfying life.

ACTION STEP

Think of a time when you thought that it was too late to make changes that you wanted to make in your life. What change in your life have you dismissed or delayed because of your age, your circumstances, or your vocation? No matter how old you are, no matter where you find yourself in life, it is not too late to do what you want to do. Find some small step today to get yourself back on the right track.

87

Schoolyard taunts have a way of sticking with us through the years and even through the decades. Once we become adults, though, it is high time to put all that behind us, to forget Becky or Wendy or Jake or whoever it was who said those mean things. When you think about it, it is really pretty sad to live life as a reaction against what happened in junior high.

At a certain point, and who knows when it happens (why not today?), we can stop trying to prove ourselves, stop trying to score points and just relax. Some people try to prove themselves by earning lots of money, others by collecting lots of university degrees, others by being extremely altruistic or religious. There are many ways of demonstrating that we are better than other people, many ways of setting ourselves apart from the crowd. There is nothing wrong with this as long as we are doing what we really want, but it becomes toxic when we take a path in life just to feel superior.

Of course, our motivations are never entirely pure. It is possible to do something both because it is really what we want to do and because we want to be better than others. To live a more abundant life, we need to gain clarity about our own motivations, to understand exactly why we do what we do. We will still make mistakes, but understanding ourselves better leads to a slight space of maneuverability, where we question our own motives and make adjustments accordingly.

Becky and Jake aren't here now; they're off in Scranton or Toledo or wherever, having babies and drinking martinis or who knows what. The fact is that we don't really have much of an audience for the choices that we make. Most people don't really care what we do. Oh, they might be interested in a juicy bit of gossip, but that's pretty much just entertainment, like reading the comics in the paper or doing crossword puzzles. Since nobody really cares, we might as well just please ourselves. We really have nothing else to do other than be ourselves, and that is work enough for one lifetime.

ACTION STEP

Do you have a little voice of criticism in your head, maybe a person from your past who still haunts you? Have you been living your life as a reaction against what that person might think?

Try today to see what it feels like to not care what anyone thinks, or at least try to imagine what that would be like.

88

Louise Hay, one of the founders of self-help and positive psychology, wrote that "the more self-hatred and guilt we have, the less our lives work. The less self-hatred and guilt we have, the better our lives work, on all levels....Guilt always looks for punishment, and punishment creates pain." Most of us have tried the route of guilt and self-hatred, and we keep doing it, even though that route doesn't work. Mindfulness practice teaches us to catch ourselves in the act, to see that negative self-talk and take a step backward.

Punishing ourselves is like trying to rebuild a house while continually demolishing our progress. At some point, we have to put down the sledgehammer and get out the framing hammer. We have to construct a new self out of the wreckage of the past. And it's never too late, no matter how many years have gone by. We can overcome the damage from past relationships, the ravages of addiction, the deficits from poor financial decisions, the bad health from past neglect. As soon as we start to love and care for ourselves, the healing begins.

We slowly begin to believe that we deserve the good things that life has to offer. We are worthy of love and respect in our relationships. We are worthy of good work that is well compensated. We deserve the care that we put into our bodies, from diet and exercise to clothing and grooming. We deserve time for ourselves, to meditate, write, and pursue hobbies. We deserve to be happy and fulfilled. This feeling of being worthy magnifies the good coming into our lives and prevents the destructive patterns from returning.

We stumble along the way and slip backward sometimes, but our trajectory is upward, toward greater peace and contentment. Each day brings another opportunity to build on solid ground, to make sound decisions in keeping with health and abundance. The sad, old days of guilt and self-hatred fade away, and we come to love and cherish ourselves. This new self now emerging will be different. We will look better and feel better. We will have more energy and enthusiasm, and we will enjoy each new day in this new life.

ACTION STEP

What habits of self-punishment do you still have in your life? Do you have issues around food or self-harm, drugs or alcohol? Do you stay in destructive relationships? What would it mean for you to commit to a major change today? Pledge right now that you will love yourself no matter what, that you will put health and healing first.

89

In a downhearted mood, it can feel like everything is going wrong, like your life is a disaster. Practicing gratitude is one way to turn that dynamic around. As you complete the gratitude practice every day, you begin to realize that more is right with your life than is wrong with your life. You see more places of strength than places of weakness. You see more possibility than you do limitation. The problems that seemed so large and uncontrollable begin to seem well within the scope of your capacities.

Instead of focusing on what you do not have, focus on what you do have. Instead of concentrating on what you cannot control, concentrate on what you can control. Instead of focusing on limitation, focus on capabilities. Your ego self will rebel against this approach; it will grumble and complain. After all, your ego does not want change. But eventually, with repeated practice, the ego self will fall into line and even dissolve entirely.

You can have the life of your dreams, but you have to be willing to make the inward shift toward gratitude. Gratitude makes you more aware of the resources available to you. And you have to first be aware of the resources available to you so that you can take better advantage of them. Gratitude helps you to gain traction and move forward in life. It helps you to get out of the places where you feel stuck and begin to make positive changes.

Each and every day is a chance to begin anew, to press the reset button. Gratitude is one way to put a close on the old ways of being and start a new approach to life. Gratitude does not happen automatically. Like anything else that you do, you have to *practice* gratitude, to make it part of your approach to life. Each day you have a choice: to be crabby and disgruntled or to make your peace with life. Gratitude is one way to make peace in your life—both within your own mind and in your relationships with others.

ACTION STEP

What is holding you back from practicing gratitude? See if you can identify some of the excuses that your ego mind has presented. Are you afraid that the gratitude exercise is a waste of time? Do you tell yourself that it does not work? Do you tell yourself that you have nothing to be grateful for? Take note of the excuses and go ahead and practice gratitude anyway. Gradually you will begin to feel the resistance fade.

90

You have come to the end of the ninety days of this challenge. You went outside and exercised every day. You took control of your diet. You practiced gratitude and visualization. You found more satisfaction on the job and in your relationships. Most likely, some parts of your life moved forward by leaps and bounds, but other areas still need a lot of work. Regardless, you have seen what is possible when you diligently dedicate yourself to seeking change in your life.

You have done the inner work of accepting responsibility for your current life, and you have aligned your thoughts, feelings, and actions toward creating the reality that you want. You have stopped the bad habit of blaming others for the things that go wrong and have lived a life of bold experiment, taking it upon yourself to life in a more dynamic way. You have broken out of the mold of societal expectations and lived the life of your choice, unhindered by the prospect of disapproving glances and caustic comments.

Maybe you didn't do this challenge perfectly. You may have screwed up on some days. You got down in the dumps, skipped days of exercise, and cheated on your dietary goals. But the main point is that you were willing to give this Boundless Life Challenge a chance. You took a risk by picking up this book and seeing what it was all about. Even more than that, you put some of these suggestions to work in your life, based on nothing more than a hunch that you needed some kind of change.

You have seen through these weeks that amazing things can happen when you set your heart and mind on goals of your own choosing. You have felt the power of daily discipline and positive mindset, and you see at least the first inklings of a new life beginning to dawn. You have no desire to go back to the old ways of powerlessness and resignation. You resolve today to make the boundless life your goal from this day forward. You recognize that you have everything you need to confidently live the life of your dreams.

ACTION STEP

Congratulations on making it through this challenge! Reward yourself by going on a trip, buying yourself a new outfit, or just taking a nap! Be sure to check out the suggestions in the next part of the book on making permanent changes in your life.

PART 3

FROM 90 DAYS TO 365 DAYS AND BEYOND

You made it through the ninety days of this challenge. Congratulations! You learned more about yourself, placed an emphasis on proper diet and exercise, and expanded your sense of possibility for your life. Now that you have made it to the end of the ninety days, you want to keep this good trend going. This last section of the book will facilitate the transition from new habits to lasting habits, from short-term change to life-long change. The boundless life will be yours, not just for a season but from this day forward.

CONTINUE TO FOCUS ON ACTION, NOT COMPLAINING

People absolutely love to complain. They complain about the weather, about the boss, about the amount of work they have to do. But complaining is not constructive behavior. It aims at tearing down something old rather than building something new. No matter how much moaning you do, you still will not have created the reality that you want. For this reason, the boundless life will have to be one of minimal complaining.

If you find yourself grousing about something, try to make it a habit to tie that complaint to some constructive action item. For example, if I am upset that I gained five pounds over the holidays, I could use my diet-tracking app on my phone or actually run the half marathon that I have been planning. If I find myself complaining to my neighbor Bob about my cable bill, I could instead call my cable company and ask for a better rate or just cancel my cable altogether. Or if I feel that I have too many responsibilities at work, I could go to my supervisor and negotiate for a reduction of duties.

As you move beyond ninety days, see if you can keep your list of complaints short and your list of your action items longer. The big, broad action items are taking time for gratitude, practicing visualization, eating a healthy diet and exercising daily, and trying new things and having a good time with life. These are the suggestions in this book that pertain to everyone, but you have action items that are unique to your own life. If you don't know what your action items are, your complaints can actually be a pretty good guide. Just take your complaint and convert it into an action. If you keep doing this on a repeated basis, it actually transforms the conditions on the ground and gives you a life that is more enjoyable.

MAINTAIN YOUR HEALTHY HABITS

Sometimes when we hear health advice, it goes in one ear and out the other. We are exposed to a lot of conflicting information, and we have to contend with companies purveying products with what may be magical health and wellness claims. It can be hard to detect the truth in all of the noise. We know that we are supposed to exercise and eat a healthy diet, but, beyond that, the specifics often get lost. All of us probably want to be able to tackle life with more energy, to lose weight, and to be faster and stronger. At the same time, we don't want crazy-making advice that turns health into an obsession. We need simple, clear rules that anyone can follow.

We are willing to exert some effort, but we don't want a 24/7 preoccupation with monitoring our daily routines. After all, we need to earn a living. We have to take care of kids and companion animals. And we want to have fun along the way as well. I believe that we can live healthier lives while still keeping a busy schedule; we don't have to choose between wellness and work. In fact, taking care of personal fitness leads to more creative and energetic work. The time that we take to go to the gym, to eat a decent meal, or to do some meditation more than pays for itself in the form of higher quality of life and higher quality of work. As we begin to cultivate the practices outlined in this book, we will be able to achieve more in less time, as we make better and more efficient choices.

Diet

In the area of diet, try to the best of your ability to eat whole foods. Prioritize whole grains over processed grains. Avoid fried foods as much as possible. Eat minimal amounts of sugar. Eat a lot of fruits and vegetables. That's it: the whole food plan in a nutshell.

Consider Vegetarianism

Beyond that, if you want to push yourself, you might consider a vegetarian diet. Why? Well, there are plenty of ethical reasons. But the health considerations are also too important to ignore. According to the Physicians Committee for Responsible Medicine, a vegetarian diet, combined with regular exercise, can reduce the risk of heart disease, lower blood pressure, reduce or eliminate diabetes, and prevent kidney stones. Following along with utilitarian philosophy, I like to suggest reduction of harm and not complete abstinence. In other words, it's better to reduce meat intake if you can't get all the way to completely eliminating it. The vegetarian equivalent of a big compendium like *Joy of Cooking*—the cookbook *How to Cook Everything Vegetarian* by Mark Bittman—will show you how to make a vegetarian version of any old favorite you want to make.

Most people worry about protein when they hear about switching to vegetarianism. But there are plenty of vegetarian sources of protein, such as quinoa, black beans, chickpeas, and even spinach! Most Americans eat far more protein than their bodies need, most of it in the form of meats, increasing risk of heart disease, diabetes, and cancer.

And, to address another potential argument, vegetarian diets do not have to be bland or tasteless. In fact, vegetarian eating can be quite adventurous if you make forays into Middle Eastern, African, Caribbean, and Asian cuisines. All sorts of interesting fusion cuisines become possible when world cultures interact in the kitchen. (Check out the wonderful cookbooks *An Invitation to Indian Cooking* by Madhur Jaffrey, *Vegetarian Dishes from My Korean Home* by Shin Kim, and *Afro-Vegan: Farm-Fresh African, Caribbean, and Southern Flavors Remixed* by Bryant Terry for ideas.) Eating a vegetarian diet can get you excited about trying new foods and brushing up on your culinary skills. It takes you to farmers' markets and specialty shops and gets you trying new restaurants and new ingredients.

Eat Enough Fruits and Vegetables

The familiar USDA food pyramid recommends two to four servings of fruit and three to five servings of vegetables per day. The majority of Americans, as well as those in most other Western nations, fall short of these recommendations. Yet incredible health improvements are completely possible with ordinary foods. Fruits and vegetables, as long as they are not prepared by frying or with excessive fats and sugars, are great for making you feel full without a ton of calories. But to get the necessary servings, it will be necessary to front-load vegetables. By this I mean eating some fruits and vegetables in the a.m. hours, by having a midmorning snack that includes fruits and vegetables. We cannot afford to wait until dinner to eat fruits and vegetables. Lunch must go from being a quick expedient of meat and fries to a beneficial platter of fruits, vegetables, beans, legumes, and whole grains.

Exercise

In the area of exercise, try to exercise seven days a week for about an hour a day. This will feel like a huge time suck at first, like a big commitment, but it will get results in a way that the half-hearted efforts do not. In order to see the change that we want to see, whether it's weight loss or increased strength and stamina, we have to put in the effort required.

Be sure to vary the type of exercise you do; in fact, cross-training is a must. The more different types of activity you have at your disposal, the more likely you will be to avoid repetitive motion injury, which can derail progress. Have at least two days with something low impact, like swimming or yoga.

Let me say a word about intensity. You can get really high-grade graphs and data from fitness trackers these days, but sometimes this can be too much information, especially when you are first beginning to get into a fitness regimen. Supposing you are very sedentary and have not done an hour of exercise in many years, start with just walking. If you need to rest, stop for thirty seconds at most. Then you might try walking for three minutes and resting for thirty seconds. Or, supposing you can walk for an hour but not run for an hour, you might run for three minutes and then walk for thirty seconds. Gradually you begin to build your capacity, so that you can hold a faster pace without breathing any harder. This is the exact same process that elite athletes use to build stamina and endurance; they alternate periods at higher intensity with periods of lower intensity. Don't determine effort by distance but by the rate of breathing and heart rate. Use a heart rate monitor if you like, or simply estimate by perceived difficulty. As the days and weeks go by, you will more easily get through the hour of exercise and see dramatic improvements in your fitness level.

As a general rule, make sure to have a warmup and cooldown on either end of the workout, lasting five to ten minutes. Then you should have a block of moderate intensity (50%–60% effort) and a block of high intensity (70%–80%) sandwiched in between. That can be broken down in millions of different ways, but most programs have this combination of light, moderate, and high intensity. Assuming it's not freezing cold outside, you know your body is warm when you begin to sweat. You know you have reached moderate intensity when you are beginning to breathe more rapidly but can still hold a conversation. You know you have reached high intensity when you are breathing heavily and can only say a word or two at a time.

The last part of the exercise portion of the challenge is to build toward a goal, like a 5K or 10K race, a swim of a particular distance, say 1,000 or 2,000 meters, or a 12- to 20-mile bike ride. Or, for yoga, you could aim for a dozen sun salutations in a row. Having a date on the calendar with a goal attached to it makes it easier to get motivated for the daily training, and, if you have to put down some hard-earned cash for equipment and entry fees, you are more likely to follow through. Don't be worried about being competitive; in most fitness events, there will be a large contingent of beginners. The most important thing is to hit the goals that you set for yourself. Everything else is just icing on the cake. Control what you can control: your daily training. Worry about the process, not about outcomes. If you build good habits into your lifestyle, everything else will follow.

INCORPORATE MORE FORMALIZED MEDITATION

At some point, you may want to embark on a more formalized program of meditation. You will want to find a teacher or a school of meditation that fits with your values. I currently practice Shakti inner yoga and read Vedanta philosophy, but you may feel more drawn to Zen Buddhism or Christian contemplative prayer. Of course, we also go through different seasons of life and may try multiple paths at various points. It is important to drink deeply of the traditions in which you engage and have more than just a cursory understanding of the philosophy behind the practice. There is little danger in overdoing it as long as you keep the other aspects of your life on track (relationships, career, finances, etc.). Having a program of spirituality makes life feel more full and rich, and we can all benefit from some formal instruction.

These days, we have a wealth of materials available to us at a moment's notice. The philosophical and religious texts of the entire world can be downloaded in five minutes. Through the Internet, we can join communities half a world away. This is a great gift, but it can also be overwhelming. If you are feeling lost, remember to go back to the inner guide. The right teacher will appear when you are ready. The right books will appear when you are ready. Simply follow the steps as they occur to you, and you will soon find yourself making progress by leaps and bounds.

ENVISION A DIFFERENT KIND OF FIVE-YEAR PLAN

The life that you have now springs naturally from the choices that you made over the years. You are the beneficiary of the thousands of small decisions made by your past self. Some of those past actions have already borne fruit, while others may bear fruit in the time to come. Either way, you have your present life by virtue of your past and the ways that you have interacted with the people and circumstances in your life.

Given this structure of time, that you select your own inheritance by what you choose to do today, think about what kind of life you would like to have a year from now, five years from now, and ten years from now. What kind of physical health would you like to have? What would you like your body to look like and feel like? What kind of house would you like to live in? What kind of job would you like to have? Give yourself the freedom to fantasize a bit about your ideal life. Try not to place any restrictions or limitations; just imagine what your life would look like in the best of all possible worlds. Fantasize using all of your senses, and make your vision as real as you can make it in your mind's eye.

Once you have used your imagination as much as possible, get out a pen and paper and see what you would have to do now to have the sort of life you would like to have in the future. Try to take luck out of the equation as much as possible; winning the lottery, for example, should not be on your list, because this outcome does not lie within your control. You may assume a reasonable rate of return on investments, but do not put anything magical in your plan. Think about the kind of lifestyle that you need to have for good health, the sort of savings and investments you need to make, the ways that you need to maintain your relationships, the steps that you need to take to advance your career. The point is to see that your ideal life may be closer than you think and that you can do things now to affect its arrival.

You create your own future every single day through the things that you do with your time and money. Some choices only affect the next five minutes, and some will have long-term effects, lasting years or decades. We live in the wake of the choices that we made in the past, which means we have to learn to be kind and generous toward our future selves. And we also want to have lots of fond memories to look back on, so we should be wary of delaying all gratification. A good life has a balance of enjoying things now but also planning for the future, a balance that allows us to live with as little regret as possible.

EMBRACE THE VIRTUOUS CYCLE OF BELIEF

The *virtuous cycle of belief* refers to the process of deliberately believing that a better life is possible and taking the daily steps necessary to maintain that positive frame of mind. Even the most hard-boiled pessimist (and I used to be one of those people—still am on some days) can be positive for five or ten minutes. Extending the virtuous cycle of belief requires a daily program of self-discipline like the one outlined in this book: practicing gratitude and visualization, taking care of mental and physical health, and pushing boundaries by challenging yourself in all areas of life. As you regularly practice the discipline of looking for the positive, you gradually move your life to a better place, a place where you can more fully be yourself without constantly worrying about little daily hardships.

When you believe in the possibility for a brighter future, you set into motion a mental state of affairs that looks for confirming instances. If I think that today will be a really lucky day, lo and behold, someone pays for my coffee unbeknownst to me, a check arrives in the mail, and I seem to be getting along better than usual with my partner. If I carried around a rabbit's foot or a four-leaf clover on my lucky day, my good fortune could easily be chalked up to superstition and co-incidence. But if I deliberately cultivate a good pattern of belief, and then I follow that good pattern of belief with positive actions, I begin to move outside the realm of luck. If I make my own luck through my actions, it is no longer fair to just say that good fortune smiled on me. The boundless life is all about claiming the power that you have in your thoughts, feelings, and actions. You then develop a positive feedback loop, where good thoughts lead to spotting opportunities where you previously only saw a monotonous existence. You leverage these opportunities through positive efforts. Some of these efforts lead to immediate payoffs, while others take longer to mature. Regardless of whether the rewards come right away or do not appear to be materializing at all, you can stick to doing your part and taking care of what you can control.

LIVE LIKE A CHAMPION

Another way to continue living your boundless life beyond the ninety days in this book is to think of yourself as a championship athlete. No, you don't need to be an Olympian, but you do need what I call every-day athleticism: not necessarily competing against other people but trying to meet and surpass your own goals. A boundless life comes from finding that inner resolve, the will to cut through challenges and obstacles, to stop settling for less than the best. If you allow this championship spirit of resolve to transform everything that you do, whether it's going on an early morning run or planning a menu for the week or letting go of bad habits, you're saying that you have faith in yourself and believe that you are worth the effort that it takes to live in a more healthy manner.

There will be many times when it will feel like the world is working against your newfound habits. The giant cheeseburger advertisement on a billboard will call out to you. Maybe you have a huge pile of paperwork dumped on you at work, which tempts you to skip that afternoon walk. Or maybe you have people in your life who constantly try to derail your efforts. When these sorts of pressures come your way, remain firmly fixed on your goals. Dig deep inside and find that wellspring of resolve and discipline. Begin thinking of yourself as a champion, and you will become a champion. Think of yourself as an athlete, and you will become an athlete. Allow those good habits to transform you, one day at a time. Each workout builds on the one before, and you steadily make progress toward a better life. The dietary choices that were hard in the beginning get easier. You find yourself craving healthy foods and looking forward to your daily workouts. You enjoy looking and feeling better, and you can't wait for more transformation to take place in your life.

We can't all be professional athletes, but we can all improve our performance in life. We can get faster, stronger, and better at what we do. The increased energy that we receive from physical activity can be put to work in all areas of life. We find ourselves more cheerful and peppy on the job, less annoyed at the pesky everyday details, and more contented with friends and family. Plus, when we take care of ourselves, we become more able to take care of others. We no longer work from a place of resentment but are able to give freely, knowing that we have done everything we could do to ensure our own wellbeing. When we begin with the mindset of a champion, we can translate that energy and enthusiasm into all aspects of life.

CONCLUSION

Embracing the boundless life means holistically taking care of your well-being. You'll become a happier person as a result of your quest for the boundless life. You are no longer so down in the dumps when things don't go exactly according to plan. You have the reserves of energy that you need to tackle every challenge. You have found the true source of strength and creativity within your own soul. You know that what you put into the world returns to you, and so you never run out of ideas, never run out of resources, and never run out of love. Gone are the old days of feeling sorry for yourself and wallowing in sadness. You claim your true power as a creative being to live the boundless life—a life of joy, abundance, and freedom.

APPENDIX A
Challenge a Friend & Completing the Challenge in Groups

The Boundless Life Challenge can be completed in a solitary manner, but it can also be a group activity if you prefer. Sharing the challenge with a group of like-minded friends provides some accountability and encouragement that will make it easier to get through the ninety days and will provide some support when obstacles arise. A Boundless Life Challenge group can be formed anywhere: at your school or university, in your faith community, in your neighborhood, or at your gym. People from all walks of life and all backgrounds can benefit from this challenge, and it can be beneficial and enriching to have a diverse gathering, so as to learn from many perspectives.

You can form your group by reaching out on social media, posting a flyer, or simply asking people you already know. The size of the group should be small enough so that everyone has a chance to speak at each meeting, no larger than twelve to fifteen people. Any more than that, and you might want to split into two groups. Smaller groups are also fine; it can be more intimate to have just a pair or maybe four to six. As far as responsibilities go, you will want someone to act as an organizer, to call and run the meetings; someone to act as timekeeper, to keep things on schedule; and perhaps a scribe, to record weekly goals.

As for the format, lots of possibilities can work, but I would suggest a meeting time of an hour to an hour and a half. You may choose to meet weekly, biweekly, or monthly. At the first meeting, introduce yourselves. Then you will want to do some sort of simple opening meditation: you can find plenty of these in my other books, such as *A Mindful Day*. Then go around the circle, with each person sharing. On the first time around the circle, each person should share the progress that they have made in fulfilling the objectives of the challenge. On the second time around the circle, each person should establish concrete goals for what they want to achieve by the next session. These can be recorded in a shared notebook or file so that everyone can remember what they wanted to achieve.

A few ground rules should be established. The tone of the conversation should be kept positive: there should be no kvetching and complaining. If someone has a specific problem, it should be offered in the spirit of genuinely seeking help and feedback from the group members. If someone asks for advice but is not yet willing to hear any suggestions, the group should move along to the next person. Next, care must be taken so that one person does not monopolize the meeting time. Every single person in the group should talk at every single meeting. Whoever is running the meeting must have enough fortitude to guide the conversation.

A group can run for ninety days and then disband, or it can be kept going on a rolling basis. One person might be on day thirty and another person on day seventy-two; that doesn't really matter. In fact, it can be good to have people present at different stages, which allows everyone to benefit from the collective experience. Groups can also swell and contract in size, and leadership can change over time, or responsibilities can be rotated from meeting to meeting. You may also wish to have some strictly social gatherings, by going dancing, going out to eat, or going to see a movie. These should be held in addition to the sharing meetings and not in place of them.

As you go through this challenge, be open to inviting others who might benefit. There is no need to be pushy or use sales tactics—you will know when the time is right. A certain person's face will simply pop into your mind when you are completing these exercises, or perhaps someone will ask you where you found your sudden burst of energy. Feel free to share and challenge others. As more people practice the habits recommended in this book, the easier it gets for everyone to get in shape and live a more fulfilling life. You may also wish to document your progress by creating a blog or sharing on social media; just avoid the infamous humblebrag and try to share only with those who you think will be interested.

Above all, try to have fun with it! You might want to give your group a wacky name and wear the same silly outfits to the local 10K. Don't make the experience cult-like and insular. Welcome people who are just curious or who maybe only want to attend one or two meetings. Making new connections is part of the experience, so the more the merrier! As your group comes together, you will create positive feedback loops that make it much easier to live the boundless life.

APPENDIX B
Additional Resources

Baker, Sarah R. "Dispositional Optimism and Health Status, Symptoms and Behaviours: Assessing Idiothetic Relationships Using a Prospective Daily Diary Approach." *Psychology and Health* 22, no. 4 (2007): 431–455.

Beattie, Melody. *The New Codependency: Help and Guidance for Today's Generation.* New York: Simon & Schuster, 2009.

Bittman, Mark. *How to Cook Everything Vegetarian: Simple Meatless Recipes for Great Food.* Hoboken, NJ: Wiley, 2007.

Csikszentmihalyi, Mihaly. *Flow: The Psychology of Optimal Experience.* New York: Harper, 2008.

Goleman, Daniel. *Emotional Intelligence: Why It Can Matter More Than IQ.* New York: Bantam, 2006.

Grof, Stanislav. *Healing Our Deepest Wounds: The Holotropic Paradigm Shift.* Newcastle, WA: Stream of Experience Productions, 2012.

Hay, Louise. *You Can Heal Your Life.* Carlsbad, CA: Hay House, 2004.

Hollis, James. *Finding Meaning in the Second Half of Life: How to Finally, Really Grow Up.* New York: Penguin, 2005.

Irwin, Bill, and David McCasland. *Blind Courage.* Waco, TX: WRS Pub., 1996.

Jaffrey, Madhur. *An Invitation to Indian Cooking.* New York: Knopf, 1973.

Kim, Shin. *Vegetarian Dishes from My Korean Home: Flavorful Korean Recipes in Simple Steps.* New York: Banchan Story, 2016.

Kondo, Marie. *The Life-Changing Magic of Tidying Up.* Berkeley, CA: Ten Speed Press, 2014.

Kostka, Tomasz, and Violetta Jachimowicz. "Relationship of Quality of Life to Dispositional Optimism, Health Locus of Control and Self-Efficacy in Older Subjects Living in Different Environments." *Quality of Life Research* 19 (2010): 351–361.

Kuhn, Thomas S. *The Structure of Scientific Revolutions*. 3rd ed. Chicago: University of Chicago Press, 1996.

Lester, Meera. *Rituals for Life: Find Meaning in Your Everyday Moments*. Avon, MA: Adams Media, 2017.

Nikhilananda, Swami. *The Gospel of Sri Ramakrishna*. New York: Ramakrishna-Vivekananda Center, 2007.

Noddings, Nel. "Caring." In *Voices of Wisdom: A Multicultural Philosophy Reader*, edited by Gary E. Kessler, 107–118. Belmont, CA: Wadsworth, 2010.

Same 24 Hours, The. Podcast with Meredith Atwood. https://thesame24hours.podbean.com/.

Seligman, Martin E.P. *Learned Optimism: How to Change Your Mind and Your Life*. New York: Vintage, 2006.

Thug Kitchen. *Thug Kitchen: The Official Cookbook: Eat Like You Give a F*ck*. New York: Rodale, 2014.

Tillich, Paul. *The Courage to Be*. New Haven, CT: Yale University Press, 1952.

Zeiger, Joanna. *The Champion Mindset: An Athlete's Guide to Mental Toughness*. New York: St. Martin's, 2017.

INDEX